"The crimes are pure H.P. Lovecraft, and the author catches this element with great skill. An excellent and absorbing work which deserves to be popular, particularly with the young."
COLIN WILSON - True Crime expert, author/co-author of "Written in Blood", "The Serial Killers", "The Encyclopaedia of Modern Murder" and "A Criminal History of Mankind".

"It is a compelling/repellent tale, told here with a certain amount of wry, if black, humour. Well-researched and insightful."
THE DARK SIDE

"... PSYCHO! is deliberately written like a novel, and is all the better for it. Woods writes at full throttle, rattling through his story like a train about to crash off the rails...
Top grade depravity, not to be missed."
DIVINITY

"Long before Jeffrey Dahmer, there was a pioneer whose "work"
helped to inspire my films. You might believe P.A. Woods was eyewitness to his crimes...
CORPSE-F---ING GREAT!"
JORG BUTTGEREIT, director of the notorious NEKROMANTIK movies

ED GEIN - PSYCHO!
by
Paul Anthony Woods
ISBN 1 897743 00 9
Copyright (c) Paul Anthony Woods 1992
All rights reserved.
Original edition published 1992
by
Annihilation Press (a division of Creation Press)

This revised and extended edition published by
by
Nemesis Books
Unit 4 - Millmead Business Centre
Mill Mead Road
London N17 9QU.
(Tel. 081 - 880 - 3925/Fax 081 - 801 - 0179)

MANY THANKS TO:

Bal Croce
Lux & Ivy of The Cramps
Rick Veitch (& the artists of Bad Trips)
UNGAWA!
James Havoc
Damon Fox
Roger Armstrong (of Big Beat)
Nick Garrard
David Elliott (of Tundra)
All were instrumental in providing source material for this book.

Stills/photographs taken from private collections,
and by courtesy of:
New Line Cinema
AIP
Analysis Film Releasing Corp.
Studio One
Wide World
UPI

The representation of Ed Gein's religious and sexual mania, in this book, was partly
inspired by David Slater's article,
"Touched by the Left Hand of God", which appeared in Headpress issue no. 2.

Part One
THE WOMANSKINNER OF WISCONSIN

The following story is not told in documentary fashion.
In using the known facts about the case of Edward Gein,
the author has attempted to get to the dark heart of the matter.

PROLOGUE:

"Get your hat now, Eddie. The sherrif's car's here to run you over to the courthouse." The busy little guy stopped fussin' with his thin hair. Pudgy frame almost sleek in a thin-lapelled 1950's jacket, he straightened his Slim Jim tie an' made to the corridor, never takin' his eyes from the floor. He knew ev'ry inch of that place. Never had to raise an eye to avoid collidin' his furrowed forehead with the wall. In all his years there, he'd performed every functional task he could - cleaned the floors, pushed trolleys, served the food. He'd even made a few of the chairs, though nowadays his upholstery material was of a less organic kind.

It was a repetitive existence, though not necessarily a bad one. His room was small an' warm. He satisfied his sweet tooth with the tiny allowance they paid him for his work. There was a TV, and radio, shared by all of the inmates. And, best of all, there were regular meals - hot meals. A body can't undervalue the worth of three meals a day, he told himself, tuckin' his curved belly into the one-button jacket.

But a grown man has other needs. That was the truth of it. As the nurses handed him to the care of the Waushara County sheriff, he kept his ears attuned to the outside world. Not a heck of a lot goin' on - a few crickets chirruppin'. The distant flap of a hawklet's wings.

But it never takes much to make a man desire freedom. That's the whole heart of the matter, he told himself - only nat'ral for a body to want to go someplace. And in an institution like Central State, you only got told No, you couldn't go **any**place. In the back of the police car, he raised his eyes to the middle distance of the sky. Listened hard to the sounds 'a freedom, though they were less distinct beneath the rattle of the engine. The air was still. It was summer, no icy whistle in the air. Not like the way he remembered back home. There, out in the solitude of the woodlands, the wind carried ugly, shrieking voices on the breeze.

Chapter One
HARD TIMES IN GOD'S OWN COUNTRY
"Mary, take the baby,
the river's risin'.
Muddy water takin' back the land."
- John Bundrick

If anything ever portended grimly for the future of George
Gein an' his family, it was his own sad beginnin's. Back in
Vernon County, as a small boy, he'd been part of a reg'lar family. Things seemed secure, permanent, though they were never
more than a buck or two ahead of the local church mice. Then
one day, back in the 1880's, Ma, Pa an' Sis went off to trade at
the market. Supplies were low as they get, and George'd been
left behind to take care of the chickens, in case the risin' Missis-
sippi river should sweep through and leave 'em mud-caked. It
did much more than that.

The Gein family, 'ceptin' their only son, never came home. Plain
an' simple, no goodbyes. They just upped, left, an' got swal-
lowed by the river. Left little George an orphan, longin' for the
kind of stability he'd known only a few short years.

He grew up, as even sad, lonely little boys are liable to do, and in
the fullness of time found a wife. Her name was Augusta - she
was of German-Lutheran stock, just like him, an' was younger by
three cold winters. It's from Augusta that our story springs.
They were married in the December of '99, both in their mid-
twenties an' nearly past the peak of marryin' age. Augusta was
no beauty, but she was a handsome woman. Had a fleshy rug-
gedness born of moral fortitude, an' hefty calf muscles built for
hard labor. Her an' George were both laborin' folk, but she was
possessed of that great Protestant thrift that binds your labors to
your own personal property. But before ownership, there was the
duty of procreation to take care of.

Now, Augusta wasn't a woman to go puttin' the pleasures of the
flesh before all earthly an' moral duties. "If God had wanted us

to enjoy the filthy act he'd have made it pleasurable", she'd say, leavin' George shit-faced an' feelin' like half a man. But there were times when she'd begrudgin'ly raise her dusty ol' skirt for him. When he'd saunter back from the tavern on a Saturday evenin', soused on cheap rye an' ready to show just who was boss.

"You have your way, but you make it quick, you hear?"

"I'll have my way, an' I'll have it **my way**", George would slur before prematurely ejaculatin' himself to sleep. This was not a time when sexual fulfillment was number one on a bill of rights, y'understand.

Anyhow, it wasn't long before this heavenly union got blessed with a child. Young Henry Gein, a child born to hardship, first saw light of day in January, 1902. The Geins were now a cosy family unit. Ma was beginnin' to despise Pa, and Pa feared Ma, the strong one of the household, with a personal dread too strong to confess to. "You see your father... you see him? A man all gone to waste", Augusta instructed the infant Henry as George staggered in on payday, half his blacksmith's assistant wage all drunk away. Little Gein got accustomed to the idea of Ma bein' too formidable a bitch to mess with, as did most of the neighbors. They were livin' in La Crosse, a small town in rural Wisconsin, with nothin' to indicate the name Gein would ever mean a thing but hardship, hard work, near-poverty. Same ol' thing as thousands of fellow working Americans. While the ol' man hit the bottle, Augusta turned to the only thing in her life that offered comfort from gen'ral misery. That good ol' old-time religion. The fundamental tenets of the Lutheran faith offered a justification, a set of reasons why ev'ryday miseries had to be endured. Thrift, hard work, self denial, these were the keys to the kingdom. If man or woman weakened in their resolve to live a righteous an' true existence, then, accordin' to Augusta, they were worthy neither of salvation nor the purity of God's love. An' this accounted for most of the whole, damn, sin-soaked world.

The reason the name "Gein" has a deeper resonance was born on August 27, 1906. Baptised under the name Edward Theodore. Born under the sign of the virgin, and, if you take his word, a virgin he remained 'til the day he died.

Why Augusta an' George wanted to bring another wretched soul into the world is anyone's guess. Maybe, beneath her skin of fire an' brimstone, Augusta was still burstin' for the touch of her no-good man.

Maybe. Most likely, she decided one soul wasn't enough to help populate God's kingdom, while more than two would be too alike to those feckless Cath'lics, nothin' to do but copulate an' cry into their sacramental wine all day.

Whatever, little Eddie turned out to be the favoured one. Not favoured by nature, though. Oh, he was formed reg'lar enough, but he was a small child, physically unprepossessin'. Had a sleepy left eye, account of a fleshy cyst that weighed down the lid as he got older. But he was Ma's favourite alright. Him bein' such a dependent type, so meekly eager to please, let Augusta put all her virtue, all her sufferin', all her pain, all her misery, into this one little boy. All he required was a little of his Ma's atten-tion each day, in return for his total devotion.

From the assessment of Dr. Martin Miller, examining psy-chiatrist at   the trial of Edward Gein:
"In many ways this patient has lived a psychotic existence for many years. He has gone through with a superficial exist-ence, so that in the eyes of people around he appeared quite rational. His activities were the result of a split level of con-sciousness. In his conscious mind, his mother was "as good a woman as it was possible for a person to be." The hatred he felt, on account of her mistreatment of him, was pushed onto women who reminded him, in appearance or situation, of her."

So Ed was a mama's boy from Day One. Pa was less a father

figure than someone who skulked in the shadows, fearful of Her
venomous tongue. Henry was what older brothers were supposed
to be, but quieter than most. As the first of the young generation
of Geins, he'd cottoned on to what it took to get by in their world
- be obligin', don't have no high-falutin' ambitions, but most of
all be prepared to work your little balls down to an appleseed if
Ma requires it of you. As Ed got older, Henry taught him to fish,
how to use a hunting knife, and, after they moved out into the
great dead heart of Wisconsin, how to trap small animals.
But first, little Eddie had to start school, an' face life beyond the
reach of Ma's overall strings. The La Crosse primary school was
akin to a smalltown bible class, no more than a dozen pupils
inside its cramped perimeters. It set a pattern for the way rural
Wisconsinites lived. You grew up in each other's pockets, knew
all your peers by name, and could name an' number each one of
their families too. No room for secrets, no need to go pokin'
your nose into other people's business.
No-one got that close to Eddie, though. He was kind of an
offbeat, distant little boy. Grinned his goofy smile at ya like a
kid with no understandin' of the language you spoke. But he
spoke up when required. An' he was quicker off the mark than
some when it came to readin'. The people in storybooks seemed
to offer all the companionship his lonely little head needed. He
never had the know-how nor the knack of becomin' popular,
either with kids or teachers. By the time his family were ready to
up an' go to those bleak woodlands, the other kids had learned
how to throw insults. "Little Eddie's a milksop!", some freckle-
faced son of the soil would holler, blowin' soggy paper into
Eddie's face from a peashooter. His features would crumple up
into tears. Too soft for this world, always too soft an' too gentle.
Plainfield was a one-horse town that made La Crosse seem
metropolitan. Augusta henpecked George into investin' in a 275-
acre farm, six miles outside the town. It embodied her work
ethic: 'stead of sinkin' your trouble an' toil into someone else's
concern, how much more righteous an' enterprisin' to work your

way into the ground on your own behalf. There was space for rearin' animals, for attemptin' to coax cash crops from the mean, frosty soil, an' enough wildness surroundin' 'em to steal the most traditional kind of livin'. Deer, beer, raccoon, umpteen kinds 'a fish - the bleak dead heart of Wisconsin had enough to feed a Daniel Boone or a Davy Crockett for life. But George Gein wasn't one 'a them. Never a happy hunter, he chose the slow grind of the farm over returnin' home empty-handed to an unforgivin' wife. And, at any opportunity, he sought solace in the bottle in pref'rence to either 'a those.

Henry an' Eddie continued their schoolin' in the town of Plainfield. For the younger boy, it was much as before. The kids weren't downright cruel, but they detected a few off-key notes in Eddie, at a time an' place when eccentricity wasn't quietly toler-ated. The schoolmistress would read off down the register -

"Arkle, Bannion, Benton, Van Dirk, Eliot, Geffen..."

"YES MISS! YESS MAAM! YESMEZZ! YUSSIRR MAAM! RIGHT HERE MISS!..."

"Gein..."

"yes miszzz..."

The other kids would hoot. No matter how they laughed, little Eddie could never make his tones much brasher - not even in the way the girls could. Ah, he didn't mind so much, 'long as they never acted wicked. But with Eddie Gein, the other kids could never figure out what was cruel and what was acceptable.

Out in the schoolyard one day, Lester Hill an' one of his buddies played fastest on the draw.

"Go on Lezzter, give 'em hell!", yelled a lumberjack-shirted boy climbin' on his friend's shoulders. "Hey... what's Eddie doing here?", snickered a little girl in plaits. "Say... what do you say, Ed?", hollered the lumberjack kid, twistin' Eddie's ear 'til it turned purple. "Howsabout puttin' those milktoast paws to the test?" For all the ribbin' he took, Eddie still carried his faraway smile. "Awww, leave ol' saggy bag-eye alone. He don't mean no harm", defended the Hill boy.

Little Lester had yet to learn that words can hurt just as much as handslaps. Eddie made a chokin' noise, fixed 'tween a sob an' a sneeze. The kids thought it was some halfwit sham, 'til his cryin' got harder. Lester reassured that he didn't mean nothin', embarrassed to apologise to an oddball like Eddie. But the tears kept right on comin'. By the time he'd ran cryin' from the schoolyard, the kids had forgot him an' gone back to their game. Not even the hayride out to the farm mended Eddie's fragile feelin's. His frayed collar was wet with tears as he tried to sneak past Pa.

"Edward... the sniffle 'a that snot'filled nose tells me you bin bawlin'!", the ol' man shouted, siftin' through any grain that wasn't too full of rat crap to bag up.

Eddie turned, obedient, not wantin' Pa's voice to get any uglier. "Yessir."

"Yes sir whut?" Pa had the ghost of an empty bottle on his breath.

"Yes sir I've bin weepin'. One 'a the boys told me an awful sad story about Ol' Man Beckley, an' how he dropped dead through hearty tack."

"None of your stories, boy, I'm not askin' for one of your sissy book tales..." Pa rolled over, hoisting himself up by the kitchen workstool. He clutched little Eddie by his weak, effeminate hand. "Ain't ever seen you cry for a livin' being outside yourself... Eugene Johnson gets his head blowed clean off in a huntin' accident, an' you walk around with a big fat dumb grin on your face. Now you tell me where the tears come from."

Eddie's thin lower lip dropped in a pout. "One of the boys called me a name."

"He called you a name?"

"Yes sir. He called me a real cruel name."

Gein pushed his son away in bewildered disgust. He couldn't look at him, couldn't abide those limpid doe eyes. Eddie stumbled back against the door, not far enough from Pa's anger. The back of his father's hand made his head ring. Vibrantly, like angels playin' on tinittus harps. He felt no pain. That never came 'til later. For now, lights were brighter, distances farther, an' the sounds outside of him drowned in silence.

"Little runt - when you gonna learn you're a man, not a weepin', dickless little girl!" Pa howled his disappointment, but it never got home to Eddie. Even Ma seemed distant, as she hauled him from the floor, throwin' hateful glances at Pa from below her thick, dark eyebrows.

"Such a powerful man, such a big strong man, huh Gein? Why don't you go back into town, throw your punches at the cheats who sold you the light wheatsacks?!"

Pa told her to keep to her own damn business. If he was ashamed to have such a weak, pitiful son, it was only natural he should feel such shame. Henry pulled Ed out of the way, handin' him a feed pail to carry. Pretty soon, the bout 'tween Ma an' Pa was a free-for-all. He was a no-good, sinful sot, and the good Lord would punish him well for how he'd made her suffer. Oh yeah? - came the reply - well the Lord had just about made him suffer enough. He coulda bin happier with some two-bit whore picked up in Wautoma.

Was that so? Well, if some painted Jezebel wanted a man who was so drunk he couldn't perform his husbandly duties, she was more than welcome. Just what made him think **he** was the one trapped in this dirty, loveless marriage?

Then came the blows. It was the only way George held any authority any more. Augusta reeled back, clutching an almighty bruise, fixin' him with a righteous glare.

"Go ahead, George Gein... go ahead an' lay your animal hands on me. You think I wouldn't prefer to shelter in the bosom of the Lord?"

Augusta's holy rages always got the better of George. He'd drop his eyes in shame, feelin' yellower than his lamebrain son. One thing she'd never let him forget was that he was a failure - he'd failed as a husband, a father, was failin' as a farmer, as a human bein'. If he hadn't had her to balance their transactions, to drive a hard bargain with other smallholders an' traders, they wouldn't just be strugglin'. They'd be starvin'. He saw no escape. Neither did Augusta. If God had decreed their joinin' should make her suffer, then suffer she would. They were joined in holy matrimony, an' so they would remain. 'Til the bitter end.

At eventime, things were dif'rent. Pa hid himself in a quiet corner, or sneaked out to empty a jug in the nearest spit an' sawdust bar. The night belonged to Augusta. Wrapped in their warmest clothes, oil lamps weavin' through the darkness, she'd make the boys forget their insecurities with her tales. Wondrous stories. No shaggy dog or bugaboo tales - her biblical narratives were rich with all the glory an' all the sufferin' of the world.

"... God saw that the wickedness of man was great in the earth, and that every imagination of the thoughts of his heart was only evil continually. And it repented the Lord that he had made man on the earth, and it grieved him at his heart. And the Lord said, I will destroy man whom I have created from the face of the earth. Both man and beast, and the creeping thing, and the fowls of the air; for it repenteth me that I have made them."

Seems the Lord was sore at the old-time folks, account of their sinfulness. The way Ma told it, it was a case of cheap, painted women leading men into damnation, and worthless men spendin' all their day's labors on hard liquor. Either way, it boded ill for the future of Plainfield, far as little Eddie could see. Ma said the whole town was full of harlots, ready to bring themselves an' any damn fool who got near 'em into disrepute. The powerful way she told it, he wouldn't have bin surprised to find a great flood come hammerin' down on Plainfield that very night. Ma preached that it was as sinful a place as any on earth, and she might have filled an eight-year old boy with the fear of hellfire. But Augusta was the bedrock of little Eddie's life. She was holy. The Ma-donna. The world was a strange an' mysterious place for him, her teachin's made sense of it.

Nights could be endless in that great, bleak, woodland void.

Eddie would lay awake with nothin' but waking dreams for company, and the wheezy snorin' of Henry in the next cot. He'd listen to the howlin' wind, a louder sound than anythin' he ever knew. Louder than the dull explosions he heard when Pa lost control, an' swiped him. Louder than the distant gunshots in the winter huntin' season. Only thing it wasn't louder than was his mother's strong, soothin' voice. Sometimes, when he listened hard, the wind carried her voice to him, readin' him Bible stories, lullin' him to sleep.

Out-of-school days were spent in daydreams. He'd help brother Henry with the chores, then walk around visualisin' all the stories he knew in his head. Given half an opportunity he'd sneak into a barn, or a piece of shrubland on the edge of the woods, losin' himself in a storybook borrowed from the schoolhouse. But mostly, the days were spent lookin' forward to the night times, when Ma would get out the Good Book to read to 'em again. Ma was preoccupied in the day, so it was hard to grab her attention. She'd be hectorin' Pa, urgin' him to work faster or turn from his own chores to somethin' more urgent. He hated it, but in the morn he was too hungover an' browbeaten to throw his weight around. Time to time, they'd disappear into the big wooden out building she'd harried him into puttin' up. It was a windowless, ramshackle affair, where they kept all the meat an' grocery supplies. Grown-up rules stated that little boys were not allowed to enter, and he'd obeyed without overmuch curiosity as to why. But one particular Saturday afternoon, his parents hadn't showed 'emselves in a good while. Little Ed was eager to get through their pork an' beans supper (an' Ma's long-winded grace), yearnin' for the evenin's storytime. He walked around the dark outhouse a couplea times, knowin' they were there but afraid to disobey Her. But, after standin' in deep concentration for who knew how long, little Ed swore he could hear noises. Whinin', yelpin', maybe a chokin' - like a soul in torment not makin' too much of a fuss. Ed tried to hold his imagination, but he couldn't stop thinkin' about what the boys at the schoolhouse said - about what grown-up men an' women did when they were alone. Strange, pointless acts. Just the thought of it made him a little queasy. Could they be doin' such things now, **his** Ma an' Pa? He saw a crack in the outhouse door, not wide enough to peek through, but if he eased it open gently...

The snufflin', blood-filled snout was not what he'd envisioned. A black hog, tall enough to stare him down should it go up on hinds, was snortin' his last. The whiskered pig's face choked on his own gore, a terminal dark tear drippin' from his eye. No-one heard him, so he widened the crack of the door 'til he had the whole picture.

His Pa stood on the left flank of the animal, holdin' it steady as it died. Ma - **his Ma** - took the dominant role, pushing a long, curve-ended blade as far into that hog as it would go. He heard a rip as it ran the length of the swine's belly. Ma pulled open the skin flaps, pure business-like, workin' at the slimy, glistenin' coils inside. The hog discharged its gook an' Ma worked her way upward from the bowels, draggin' the innards into a metal tub at her feet. Both she an' Pa had long, leather aprons on. They'd started clean as whistles, but were turnin' dark red from top to toe. And it was Ma doin' all the work. He'd guessed this was how food got put on the supper table, but never had a mind to pursue the gory details. His head lightened. He felt faint - but it wasn't the spillin' of the pig that did it. He had a warm, tinglin' feelin' down below, somethin' unfamiliar.

The door swung wide, the rest of the hog's guts missed the bucket an' slopped on the floor. Ma an' Pa turned to face him. She smiled softly in a way he'd never seen her smile before. Straight at him, kinda like they were sharin' some little secret. "Well, Edward?... Does our slaughterin' meet with your approval?" She had blood an' slime smeared the entire length of her brick-built body.

"I... I think I wet my pants", was all he could answer, overwhelmed by the warmth of the emission.

Chapter Two
MAMA'S BOY GROWS UP

"Father?" "Yes son?"
"I want to kill you...
Mother... I want to..." SCREAMS!!!
- Jim Morrison

"Edward?... Are you diddlin' with yourself again?"
"No... no, Ma... I'm just reading a very fascinating article,
and..."
Rats! Caught in the bathtub with a geographical magazine! She
snatched it from his hand, lookin' at the picture of bra-less Pa-
cific islanders with wise dismay. Eddie turned red, felt his
manhood shrivel even smaller.
"These savages are the saddest of God's creatures, son. They are
prey to the base instincts we civilised folk can overcome... Do
you understand how lucky you are to civilised, Edward?"
"Sure do, Ma", he replied, balls held tight between his legs to
make 'em totally invisible. Her cold, dark eyes regarded him
with more tolerance than she reserved for most of his species.
"You know, this...", she sunk a searchin' hand beneath the bath
water. Ed cringed, tryin' to disappear into it. "... This is the
curse of Man. Just as much as that 28-day curse is eternal retri-
bution for the sin of Eve, amen."
Ed nodded his agreement quicker than a chicken pecks corn. He
rose from the tub in shame, keepin' a cold cloth tucked tight
round his shrunken modesty. "I know you don't regard lustful
folks very high, Ma... I'll always shun 'em, I'll never be one of
'em." Augusta didn't try to hide her scepticism. Her little Ed
was close to a man now, and she'd had more than a bellyful of
the weakness of men.
"If you have to touch that overripe shrimp, Edward, that's between you and the Lord." Ma was righteous, but considerate of
human failin'. Sometimes. "The sin of Onan is as nothing

19

against the sin of the fornicator and the adulteror. Now dry yourself, and get ready for service."

Ma conducted her own sermon on a Sunday morn. Sev'ral times, they'd trekked into Plainfield to attend the Methodist church, but plain to tell she didn't approve. The preacher lacked her bite, her joyous jibes against the lustful an' slothful. In the absence of a decent, God-fearing, sin-fearing, people-fearing, Lutheran church, she'd taken up her rightful mantle of spiritual adviser. And a darn fine job she made of it. Other preachers never gave Ed the fear, and the tinglin' sensatiion, that he got from her.

As he wiped his pale pidgin-chest, checking it for the first signs of hair, Ed tried an experiment. He held his "men's things" tight between his legs. Tight. Tighter. At first it felt good, and he could feel his Rod of Jesse grow a little. But soon after, the blood got cut off, he could almost believe ev'rything was cut clean away under a cold knife. For one moment, he imagined what it was like to have no man's burden - not to have touch yourself in quiet, sinful moments. If the Lord had granted him a blank hole between his legs - like the other boys said all the womenfolk had - what would that really have felt like?

Under investigation for murder in 1957, Edward Gein gave the following testimony to the District Attorney of Waushara County:
"It was sort of a sex problem... I blame all my trouble on my mother. She should have made me a girl. I almost never went out with girls. I was afraid of them. All I could think of was my mother, and how much I really loved her. I used to wonder if some kind of operation could change me into a woman. I used to read a lot in books about anatomy..."

Squeamishness can never keep a lonely soul from wonderin' about sex. Though Ed was the shy, retiring type, he could not keep his mind, nor his sleepy eye, from wanderin'. "He's doing it again, he's looking", a long-skirted high school girl would complain to her friend through gritted teeth. Back in the early 1920's, way before the birth of the "teenager", the jazz age was so far away from the rural Mid-West as to be an alien culture. Young lust was still a mysterious adventure. It might be a misplaced hand on the way home from the barn dance. Or a wet kiss in the back row of the local picture palace. Either way, it led to embarassment or enlightenment. But for young Ed, the innocent thrill of the first date, or even a kind word, was almost too much to hope for.

"Ignore him. He don't really mean no harm." The girls all knew that if they turned an' stared he'd blush, whimperin' some incoherent apology. If they got tough with him, he might even blub like a baby.

The other boys would rib him, makin' him feel uncomfortable, with their half-notions an' their bravado about initiation into the ritual. But Ed was startin' to get educated. Even though it'd be some time before he could put his book learnin' into practice, the time would come when he'd be more familiar with the female body than any of 'em. More than any of 'em could ever dream of.

As adulthood beckoned, Ed got more distant than ever from his peers. To the locals, he was just a slow boy. Book learnin' or none, they always took him at face value. Always runnin' errands for his Ma, or trailin' his brother into town like some halfwit puppydog. Folks might ask "How y'doin', Ed?" 'Stead of returnin' their greetin', he'd draw out an answer. "In myself, I'm not so bad", he'd admit after turning the question over. "My mother, on the other hand - she's gettin' these terrible muscular spasms, back of the leg. Too much time on her feet..."

Folks only spoke to Ed if they were in the mood to give a good-natured ribbin'. He took it well, there bein' no fire or malice in him. "Sleepy eye, sleepy guy", as one of 'em remarked.

Young women only talked direct to Ed if they wanted to watch him squirm an' blush. Most were too kind-natured - they had better uses for their own purtiness. But Ed was mostly comf'table around women older than himself. Matronly, child-rearin' types. There was no-one in the world Ed admired more than a clean-livin' mother. In his mind, the virginal Madonna could be 50 years old an' weigh 18 stones, long as she had the qualities he held dear.

Some of Plainfield's middle-aged women were flattered by his high regard. He had his uses too. As things panned out, Ed was not strictly indispensible back at the farm. Augusta an' Henry had enough hard work inside 'em to carry two more. So Ed was always around, to erect a fence or help with the harvest. And, best of all, you didn't always have to pay 'em. Fellow of simple tastes like him - what does he want with loose cash hangin' round his pocket? Better to feed him some buttermilk, or home-made ice cream, somethin' he'd appreciate. In fact, Ed was the all-purpose good neighbor. The ideal person to look after your kids, while you took a ride out into Waushara County or attended a local function. Sure, he'd have 'em spooked by the time you got home - he had a head full of ghost stories, all the local legends an' old wives' tales. A regular Cotton Mather. But you'd be sure they went to bed meek an' obedient, no time for misbehavin'.

Not ev'ryone took to Ed Gein, but those that did knew his quali-ties. To smalltown folks, there are certain kinds 'a behaviour that are plain intolerable: the cussedness of badmouthin' your neigh-bours, disrespect for local custom an' etiquette. Of these, Ed Gein exhibited none. People who'd grown up with him, like Lester Hill and Elmo Ueeck, knew what they were talkin' about when they said there was plenty strangeness in Ed, but not a trace of wickedness.

Back home, things were the same as ever but moreso. Food never ran out, but things were runnin' down. Gates fell off their post, the mean soil sprouted nothin' but weeds or black grass. Ma an' Henry were too busy scratchin' a livin' to bother much with details. Ed would help out, whenever he wasn't retreatin' to his private world. But as for ol' man George... His days as any kind of father figure were so far gone neither boy could clearly recollect 'em.

Whenever the farm made any small surplus, George would skim it off without much askin'. Life was bitter without the bottle, an' even with the bottle it wasn't too much better. His waverin' shadow would shatter the yellow oil light, while Augusta sat in the cool of night darnin' 20-year old undergarments. He'd look around, his lined face anticipatin' hate-filled shrieks. They never came. Henry carried on cleanin' his rifles, while Ed stuck his nose in some cockermamie book. It was like he didn't exist anymore.

"Why, thankyou, mah beloved famlee", he'd slur, "... an' a warm hullo t'you too."

Only Augusta dared answer. In advanced middle-age, her unshaken timbre carried more authority than any of 'em had ever heard.

"You're a worthless man, George Gein... Way, way below my contempt." He'd slump in a threadbare armchair, as far from her, her sewing machine an' her Bible as he could be. The boys never spoke to him these days, not at all. Lonesome Henry - ev'ry part as much the inward-looker as Ed, but without the cute eccentricities - didn't care much for a man he saw fallin' apart in front of his eyes. Neither of the boys cared for hard liquor. They had the ol' man's fine example, and the sacred word of Augusta, to thank for that. For Ed's part, acknowledgin' his Pa seemed kind of a disloyalty to Ma. 'Sides, he didn't have to worry about him rainin' slaps down any more - both the slapper an' the slapped were beyond slappin' age.

As George got weaker, through drinkin' an' gen'ral decrepitude, so Ma seemed to get stronger. In the end, he didn't have the strength (nor the money) to ramble his way down to the Plainfield tavern. He'd just sit, feedin' on a quart of rye, or some hokey cheap liquor he'd laid his hands on. The booze poured down his neck 'til it trickled back out his pores. When they were in the house together, him an' Ma were like two opposin' sides of a plate glass window: the fall of Man gazin' up pitif'ly at the Holy Madonna. They never made conversation. George's angry, ramblin' words would turn against himself, 'til he'd get round to pleadin' with himself for pity. Then one day he fell from his stool, implorin' her as he held on tight to her workin' boot: "Cold... so damn cold... help me, Auguz... Cold burnin' in my lungs... cold way down in my bones." He coughed, like he was dislodgin' a boulder from his chest. Ed kept his gaze on Ma. If there was a way to react, she'd show him. But she hardly moved at all. Pa was bathed in mucus an' sweat, despite all his talk of cold. She looked down on him with disdain.

"When any man hath a running issue out of his flesh, because of his issue he is unclean", she recited from memory. "Every bed whereon he lies is unclean; and every thing, whereon he sitteth, is unclean."

Like a true Christian soul, she mopped his suppuratin' brow with water from a rusted pan. Afterwards, she made a thorough job 'a cleansin' her work-hardened forearms.

Sure enough, Ma was right. Ol' George was unclean. Several pints a' pneumonic fluid on the lungs-unclean. The long, hard Wisconsin winter had crept under his skin, while the hooch kept his body temp'rature low. In the spring of 1940, the obituary in the local smalltown rag read:

"George Gein, 66, passed away April 1. He had suffered considerably, but his sufferings were eased by his faith in God. He was a good husband and father, and will be missed by all who knew him."

If Augusta said "Amen" to that, it'd prove even the sanctimonious know irony when it bites 'em. Local rumour had it George Gein died with a smile on his face, relieved to get out. So now, at the respective ages of 38 & 34, Henry an' Ed were fatherless little boys. They liked it that way - just them an' their dearest beloved.

Things were kept ship-shape around the farmstead. Ma had a tighter rein on the finances, an' more inclination to build on what they had. She was no longer a young woman, but she was still a backbone to her sons. If she didn't overpay Ed for his complete devotion to her... well, he knew he had her unspoken love, all the same. Her sermons on the evil of mankind (or womankind, more commonly) came less frequent, but they were still full of old-fashioned puritan commonsense - "If a woman's good enough for intercourse, she's good enough for marriage." She must have figured that, by this age, her boys had taken her warnin's to heart. They weren't the marryin' kind, leave alone the womanizin' kind. Ed's life (apart from his chores) was filled with cheap paperbacks an' cheesy magazines he bought from Wisconsin town stores. They had pretty sinful-soundin' titles - Two-Fisted Detective, Hardboiled Tales - an' the covers were full of young women with ridiculous mammaries an' low-cut dresses... but at least her boy wasn't hauntin' the bars an' whorehouses.

Henry was a dif'rent breed of loner. He'd most often be out in the woodlands, alone with his thoughts an' a host of dead critters he'd acquired. Him an' Ed had quite a collection of firearms between 'em - two .22 calibre rifles, a .22 pistol, a 7.65-mm Mauser, an' a 12-gauge shotgun. But Ed never was the huntin' type. He'd go out with Henry for a little target practice - maybe bag a few squirrels, or a big, juicy, black-eyed raccoon. Never had the stomach for anythin' bigger though - claimed he once damn near fainted, when he saw a full round pumped into a hefty buck that refused to stay down. Made him quite a laughin' stock in the Waushara County huntin' season.

Whatever, the boys had found their own way of clean livin', and were content enough for it. If they quaffed a few beers, or laughed at a dirty joke in the bar-room, Ma would never know (an' the hard stuff stayed verboten). Things were above-board an' simple at the Gein place, and it looked like that was the way they were gonna stay.

'Til one spring day in '44.

The tall, wavin' palm trees around their home could get dry as a tinderbox, on a hot summer's day. Bush fires were not uknown either, though they could gen'rally contain flare-ups in the underbrush. In Maytime, they were somethin' of a rarity, so Henry reacted slow when Ed came runnin' to tell him some trees an' shrub were goin' up in smoke.

They tried fightin' the fire, but Ed took in as much dirty smoke as from a lifetime a' Marlboros. He gave up when the suffocation was more than he could stand. Went trundlin' into town in the family's old pick-up. Never stopped to tell Ma - she was far enough from the flames to stay safe. Only person it could hurt was Henry, who, as Ed well knew, was still back in the woods. "Steady, Ed... you just keep calm awhile now." Sheriff Frank Engle had raised a small search party, along with Ed's nearest neighbors Lester an' Cliff. They trod through a dusty clearin', arid smoke hangin' in the air like the afterburn of a wild party. The flames had surely blazed through this spot, though no-one could detect 'em now. "You say you got no idea of where Henry took off to?"

"No, no, none... he just went in after the smoke." The little guy led 'em all manic'ly along, like a lemming itchin' to make his maiden dive.

"Don'tcha think it might be an idea to stop off at your place - check if he turned tail an' headed home?"

Marchin' into an ash-laden copse, they let Lester's wheezy question go unanswered. Stretched on a scorched piece 'a ground was Henry Gein. Less animated than the burnt pine trees. Woulda been out straight, if not for a slight inclination to lay on his side. Like he'd got locked in the middle of a contortion.

"No pulse... my brother's got no pulse", Ed softly testified. He was down on his knees, unlockin' Henry's tightened fist from the promise of rigor mortis. Sheriff Engle was mostly concerned with the deep purple wounds runnin' down Henry's forehead an' face. "Oh Lord above, Ed, lemme through now... Don't seem like Henry's breathin' none." He held off the urge to run his fingers down the open tramlines on his face. "Got some truly terrible burns... I'm so sorry, Ed." Burns coverin' half his head, Engle acknowledged to hisself, but none at all on his body or his clothes. Those wounds coulda just as easy been lacerations - bludgeon marks from some heated weapon. But that wasn't feasible. "Small miracle we found him at all". Cliff Bates cut the pregnant silence. "I mean, account of how you couldn't find him, before you rode over to town."

Ed nodded slow, in agreement, with a faraway look ev'ryone assumed was brought on by shock. "Funny how that works", he said.

Henry Gein was judged to have died from heart failure, effected by asphyxiation. His wounds were not profound enough to cause death, an' foul play was surely out 'a the question. At the funeral, Ed held tight to his poor ol' mother's arm, though that formidable woman didn't seem to need any support. Still, misery was workin' itself into her tough, stoical face. Her family kept on shrinkin, an' all she had left was her weak, devoted son. "I won't let anythin' else bad happen to us, Ma", Ed promised. "Not ever again." Augusta was unmoved. She had faith in God, not Man, an' even He wasn't treatin' her too kind as of late. The death of George had been tolerable. Desirable, even - it was God's will that a sinner should atone for his sins. But her eldest son - hard-workin' an' pure, just the way she'd brought him up - that was almost too hard to bear. If she didn't know how God wove his mysterious pattern into all things, she might swear it was the work of the Devil. Maybe even someone a little less grandiose, much closer to home.

"I swear, Edward, you may have some of your brother's belly for work, but you got your father's head for business." Ed took her chidin' with magnanimity. He was fixin' an' mendin' an' runnin' round more than he'd ever done - but she still gave the orders. She was the head, he the hands. In his own mind, Ed was the perfect provider, the perfect son. He was just about as happy as life would ever allow him to be.

In her old age, Augusta was findin' worries. Edward was a good son, an' a good Christian, but he was gettin' strange ideas. "Going away to your room, Edward, to read your trash?", she'd murmur with disapproval over her yellowin' ledger books.

Ed would beam his shit-eatin' smile, an' defend his choice of lit'rature. "It's very educational, Ma. This one here tells about the lives of primitive tribes in the South Seas. Truly fascinatin'..."

Augusta refused to sully her vision with such filth. "You used to love the scriptures when you were a boy, son... Why do you bother your head with this profanity?"

But alongside of her, the stuff he read was the centre of Ed's universe. Lyin' back on his ol' brass bed, he was absorbed into the world of the legendary anthropophagi. How they would gouge out the eyes of dead enemies, sew the lids, take the teeth, then subject the head to their infamous shrinkin' processes.

Damn, it was excitin' stuff! They may have been ghoulish folks, but they had talent. He read how they would make their tribal drums, by stretchin' a dead man's gut to its finest point, then wrappin' the skin around a hollow cylinder. When he pictured all of this, he left behind the grey, bleak heart of Wisconsin.

But Ed's fields of enquiry were not limited to the half-mythical world of the primitive. On tradin' visits to Wisconsin Springs, he'd found a bookshop from where a man could educate himself to the fullest degree. Bought a secondhand copy of **Gray's Anatomy**, an' a couple other titles on the human body. With a little book learnin', an' a careful study of diagrams, Ed prided himself he was becomin' quite the expert. Not that he had too much opportunity to transform the theoretical into the practical. An' then there were his casebooks about the "resurrectionists" - the graverobbers of 19th century Scotland, who'd assisted in findin' specimens for the noble Dr. Knox...

On entering the Waushara County courthouse for his sanity hearing of 1974, Ed found himself nodding to the Kentucky

Colonel features of the goatee'd Judge Gollmar. Since he'd treated him so fairly at his trial, it was like coming face to face with an old friend. "How are they treating you, back at the Central State?", the judge asked informally before proceedings got underway.

"I'm happy there", Ed nodded in consideration. "It's a good place. Some of the people there are pretty disturbed though."

There were few clouds over Ed at this time. He'd assumed the role of a quietly eccentric Jimmy Stewart type, an' his neighbors accepted him more than at any other time in his life.

There were some beginnin' to have doubts, though. The month after Henry's death, Cliff Bates hired out a few local men as threshers. Ed, ever ready to oblige, went along for a minimum wage an' however much he could eat. He'd become known as one of the most uncomplainin' an' reticent of the local labourers. He'd put in a hard day's work, then, as the hands all entered the house to eat a meal cooked by the farmer's wife, he'd hangtail to the last 'til ev'ryone found a seat. Last to be seated, last to leave. Mrs. Bates had wondered whether this lingerin' arose from a helpful inclination, or whether it was somethin' a little more dubious. While the women of the house bustled about the kitchen with dirty dishes, they'd feel that sleepy eye hoverin' over their feminine forms. Sometimes, even the little girls felt his gaze undressin' 'em, without too clear an idea as to why. For the farmer's wife, this'd be the last straw.

"All finished up with your lunch, Ed?", she'd call, a cue to snap him out 'a his dreamworld. He'd come scurryin' over with his plate, only too eager to sink his elbows into the dishwater an' wash away his sinful thoughts.

But on that June day Ed hadn't a chance to cool off his hot, dark desires. While doggedly baling up hay, his attention was grabbed by a young woman calling to Cliff. "Martha went on back to the house, Clifford... Do you think you might rub a little sun oil into

my back?" The other men grinned wide, but held their comments
'til later. Cliff an' Martha's visitor was a real babe - late twenties,
long dark hair, with the kind a' figure you might find on a statue
of a Roman goddess. Had on a big, floppy sunhat, pointed sun-
glasses, an' very little else.

"She... she's stripped down to her brassiere an' corset!", Ed
panted when she returned to her sunbed. The other guys were
bustin' a gut, though in truth he spoke out for all of 'em.

"No-oo, Ed, that's the kinda bathing suit the young women wear
these days", Cliff grimaced through his own embarassment.
"Those who have the figure for it, anyways."

"No shame", Ed reprimanded, wide-eyed. "Never seen a body
with such a lack of shame. Don't she realise what all that teasin'
could do to the baser kind of feller?". Like always, the men
didn't know how seriously to take Ed. His mouth kept up that
holier-than-thou baloney, but his wilder-than-wild grin showed
his instincts were at odds.

Cliff was just a little peeved - Ed didn't normally offer his opinions on much - an' he felt that young woman could do with some
defendin'. Her name was Connie, an' she was Mrs. Bates'
younger cousin. She had a ten-year old son named Stevie, and
yes, she was a respectable wife an' mother. Her husband was a
G.I. Joe, off fightin' in Europe, **which was more than a
pantywaist like Ed had ever done**, excused service on account
of his sleepy eye an' all...

She lived quiet an' modest, takin' care of her boy in a
neighbourin' town to Plainfield. She waited faithfully for her
man to come home - her idea of a night out was to go talk with
her friend across the street, have a cup of coffee, or maybe fruit
punch on special occaisions. She'd been followin' this homely
routine all through that twelve-month, an' she'd follow it that
very night. In future though, she'd take care to make sure her
porch door was locked tight. The age of small-town security was
comin' to an end.

Returnin' home that moonlit eve, she felt just a little spooked.

Her wooden stairs were creaky, same as always when the house was goin' to sleep. She thought she heard somethin' else - mice? - but laughed at her own silly imagination. Goin' over to the McDonalds' place to listen to **Inner Sanctum** always did make things seem eerie, but she never could resist...

She did hear somethin'. It was a coughin', or moanin', or, or... "STEVIE! OmiGod, Stevie!" The dark shape barely crawlin' along the top landing was her little boy. He tried to speak, but shuddered with pain as she snatched him up by his achin' shoulders.

By the time the doctor arrived, Connie had had time to weep over the purple bruises on his neck. Talkin' still hurt him, his breathin' was labored, though too robust to cause alarm. What destroyed Connie's faith in the universal amicability of her fellow Americans was the doc's confirmation that, yes, Stevie had been the victim of a strangulation attack. No permanent damage had been done, but time would tell how shock registered on the boy.

"Someone shook me awake", he lisped with painf'ly fragile vocal cords. "It was a man - but it was so dark, I could only see he had these weird eyes. He wanted to know where Mom was. It was important. But when I told him he wouldn't believe me. He started chokin' me, 'til ev'rything went black..."

The attacker was never apprehended. All the same, Cliff Bates and his wife never invited Ed Gein to their place again, for business or otherwise. The long years of darkness were startin' to set in for Ed.

Back at the farmhouse, the very fabric of reality was about to crumble. Later that year, the chirpy, dreamy little guy, in his left-tilted deerstalker cap, came bustlin' home with a sack full of groceries an' a headful of dreams.

"Traded the maize for a little sweetcorn, Ma... Pretty sure they done us good this time... Ma?"

No answer. Ed was quick to panic. A nervous one at the best of times, he saw no oil lamp to hold up the falterin' daylight. Just Just about picked out Augusta in the shadows. Leaned back against the bottom of her comfy chair, without the strength to raise her way back out of it.

"Ma... oh Mom... oh Mother Mary", Ed wept as he helped his wounded icon to her feet. "Tell me God ain't left us. Tell me everything's alright."

Augusta could walk, falterin'ly, with her son's assistance, but ev'rything was not alright. Her son's insistent questions were met by the quiverin', downward turn of half her face. Her left hand tried to wave, to make some mute statement, but could only shake.

At the hospital, the examinin' doc confirmed the grimly obvious. "Sad to tell you, Mr. Gein, that your mother has suffered a cerebral haemorrhage... a stroke, that is."

I KNOW what it is. What kind of damn fool do you think I am? I'm the most learned man in the accursed town of Plainfield!

"Ah gee, that... that's terrible, Doc. Is she gonna be okay?"

The whitecoat looked serious. "She may well live a comfortable life for some years to come. But not a full one, Mr. Gein. I'm prescribing total bed rest. She's going to need great care and attention. If you care to wait awhile in the reception room, I'm sure we can recommend a nurse who won't stretch your budget too..."

"We don't need a nurse!" His passive features fired up into indignation. "I can take plenty good care myself! What kind of man would I be if left care of my poor, poor mother to a stranger?"

The doc blanched, unprepared for the little guy's fury. Ed remembered himself, played nervously with his cap. "She's all I have. If I can't take care of her, no-one can."

And so it was. Ed, the faithful son, lived a life totally devoted to his befallen mother. She was his world. It made sense that he should be the one dedicated to keepin' his world alive.

But Ma was falterin' Ed could pretend she was immortal, but he couldn't make it real. Nor could he stop his dark inner world from seepin' its way to the surface.

Chapter Three
THE MARTYRDOM OF SAINT AUGUSTA

"Daddy, why - why did they kill that poor little horse?" he whimpered, but his breath failed him and the words came in shrieks from his panting breast.
"They're drunk", said his father. "Playing the fool. It's not our business. Come along!"...
Raskolnikov woke up in a cold sweat, his hair wet with perspiration, gasping for breath, and he raised himself in terror."
- "CRIME & PUNISHMENT" - Fyodor Dostoyevsky

You can't keep a righteous woman down too long. Though Ed fulfilled Ma's every wish, she didn't feel secure in the hands of her little boy. Make yourself dependent on someone who's more dependent than you, where are you then? Better to have total faith in the Lord. But she wasn't yet ready to be delivered into His arms. For now, God would help she who helped herself. By an act of iron will, Augusta had herself up an' raised in the closin' year of WWII. Not that she held with that momentous era of slaughter - it was a lot of foolishness bein' fought out half a world away. She didn't approve of goin' to war against Germany in WWI, nor would she change her views now. Conflict with the fatherland had changed the wordin' of the Lutheran service into vulgar modern English - now that God's two countries were a-warrin' again, it was proof positive there was evil abroad in the world.

Older, weaker, she still had hold of the reins tighter than ever. Ed was never seen in town without his ma along for the ride, yellin' out orders like some paralysed Greek chorus. Seemed all her illness had done was tighten her up, consolidate her power. Given time, she managed more than a few steps, an' fired her mouth loose like it was never contorted in the grip of palsy. She had to make sure no-one took advantage of her easy-goin' son.

The Gein farmhouse.

The summerhouse extension - a makeshift abattoir.

. Ah, she knew he was tryin' hard to please, an' she was tryin' to be easier on him. All the same, he'd gotten slovenly in his habits, and he was readin' more of that Detective, Horror & Cheesecake junk. Surely, if she was merciful with him, the Lord could not fail to show mercy on her?

That winter, she an' Ed walked onto the property of a man named Bill Smith, about 2-3 miles from their farm. Augusta hurtled along, unsteady but with a sense of purpose. Smith was a sullen, suspicious man, more than a little fond of drink. She'd decided Ed, the holy innocent, wasn't capable of drivin' a hard bargain with such a surly type, so she led him by the wet ear.

"William Smith! We're here to make a transaction, sir!", Augusta hollered. No sign of life on the verandah. But as she quieted her voice, a hullabaloo of shouts an' wails could be heard round by the back barn.

"Looks... looks like he's got business elsewhere, Ma", Ed murmured.

"What in blazes is that man up to now?", she stalked t'ward the source of the commotion while Ed stood shy an' static. 'Til the farmhouse swung open an' shut behind him, an' he ran for Ma's skirt tails.

Smith, in a hellish rage spawned by inner demons or some bottle spirit, lashed a small mongrel dog with a cane stick. The poor brute, some half-terrier with pointed ears, had a broken hind leg pinned 'neath Smith's boot. Ma was about to remind him that the fear of God resides even within dumb animals, when the body that fled the farmhouse swept by her.

"Chris'sakes Bill, leave him be! Little creat're like that, you've no call to beat him so!" The woman spoke with a drawl, and had long, untidy hair - one shade lighter than Ma's, but not combed back and disciplined into a bun. Almost good lookin', but with a haggard agelessness that placed her anywhere from 20-36 years. Ed saw Ma's veiny eyes grow wide, and couldn't tell if it was the girl or the sufferin' mutt that sent her speechless.

"Save yer snivellin'", Smith snarled like the bottle had released some dark, resentful genie. "Last time this furball of shit growls at me!" The cane came down, an' the animal sounded a mournful note, summonin' up the strength to die. "An' you can tell these dumb-faced Swedes to stop gawkin', or get their asses the hell off my land!"

"I'll be told no such thing!", retorted Ma, riled back to life. "I am not a Swede, and I will not be talked to in the same foul manner as this "person"!"

Smith brought the cane down hard. The dog gave up the game. Smith stared at Augusta, like he'd found an unlikely ally to help torment his woman. Ed didn't know where to bury himself, the girl looked at Ma with bewilderment an' hurt.

"If he can't talk with no decency to me, then he surely can't keep a civil tongue to you", she whispered. "... ah'm his wife."

Augusta snorted. Ed worried at the chalky pallor settin' in where flushed indignation oughta be.

"You're nobody's wife. Nobody's, an' everybody's", she almost spat. "Do I see a ring signifyin' that this man has taken you as his own? You're Smith's harlot, and he oughta treat respectable people with more respect than he does your kind!"

Smith's woman leaned her head back on a wooden post, regainin' the little composure she had. "You ain't got the right to speak to me that way... no right at all."

The cane whipped the air, but the mongrel dog was silent.

"Mama's boy... take your mad ol' lady and get on home! This ain't the time to do business."

Augusta didn't need the encouragement. She staggered over the uneven, mole-hilled ground, back to where Ed had parked the pick-up. Smith whipped one more volley of lashes into the dog's mortified hide.

"Bas-tardd!", his woman hissed, defeated an' alone. "Dirty, heartless, bastard."

"That poor, dumb brute..." Gentle Ed shook his head, helpin' his mother into the truck.

"Psshh... poor dumb nothin'. If he thought so well of her, he'd marry her. Your mother's not low down enough to tarry with the likes of her!"

It took Augusta all day an' night to stop speakin' of Smith's sinful concubine. Ed tried to rid himself of the sight 'a that sufferin' dog, an' pay attention to what she said. It relieved him to find she'd burned the hussy out of her system by the next morn. But she looked none the better for it. Her long, watchful face was drawn, as grey as the grave. That slatternly young woman was truly the whore of Babylon - she'd placed a curse of sufferin' on his own dear mother.

When her constitution didn't improve after two days, Ed prayed to his own personal God - the one inside of him - and asked Her to make everything alright. He must've prayed too late.

This time, the doctor told him he could only have faith, and ask the Lord for his mother's deliv'rance. Outside the hospital ward, Ed slumped deep into private prayer. The nurses stepped quietly by, touched by the devotion Augusta inspired in her only livin' son.

O sacred Mother of God... O Mother of all that's holy and all that's within me. Why does she have to suffer, to fight a righteous fight, and then suffer and suffer again?

Ed looked deep into his own misery for a guidin' light, but found only the nastiest kind of illumination.

Because that's the kind of filthy world you live in, Edward. You can accept it, or you can rage against it, but you have to believe it. The wicked an' corrupt will thrive, while the righteous will suffer.

Augusta was buried within the week. There was little fuss in the town, the local obituary column kissin' a curt goodbye to a sanctimonious pain-in-the-ass. At the funeral, a small gatherin' of bodies came to pay tribute, more to poor, sufferin' Ed than the woman enterin' the soil. Lester, and ol' Elmo Ueeck patted his shoulders, told him to keep his spirits up. On the last day of 1945, Ed saw the cold ground open an' swallow what was left of his external world. "She was too good... just much too good for

37

all that sufferin'", he testified to the assembled. "Don't trouble your heart any more, Eddie." Irene Hill took his hand. "She's at peace now, and nothing more can hurt her."

"Yup. She's truly at peace", blubbed a tearful Ed. "And now I'm alone. I'm truly alone in this world."

And how does a feller repair his world when it's come to an end? Mostly, he does nothin', cos that's what Ed did anyhow. With Ma gone, life was lonely, but there were fewer chores, fewer responsibilties. A guy who's only been used to doin' what he's told for nigh-on 40 years, what's he gonna do when there's no-one to push him around?

Ed found freedom, of a kind. But it was a hell of a strange freedom.

He frequented the taverns more regularly that he woulda dared when Ma was alive. Sometimes, he could put away two, hell, even three bottles 'a beer a night. An' there were the ice cream sodas. When he had a pocket loaded with small change, he could be a hog for ice cream sodas. But such reckless spendin' didn't soothe the pains of loneliness. An' so, our boy Edward found himself a girl. Almost.

Adeline Watkins was a 38-year old spinster lookin' for companionship. She was a mildly eccentric-lookin woman, in that midwestern way. No beauty queen, but not ugly either, she had a long Wicked-Witch-of-the-West nose an' wore horn-rimmed glasses. She an' Ed met in the Plainfield drug store (Plainfield is that kinda place - one church, one food store, one petrol station, an' a couplea part-time police). Ed had been out deliverin' lumber in his pick-up, the kinda casual labor he took on more frequently now. She an' Ed were sight acquaintances, just like most people in an' around town. Just two empty seats apart at the soda fountain, it didn't take long before they got around to politie conversation.

"You know what the weakness is with most American murderers?"

Adeline replied that she didn't but, would be fascinated to hear about it anyway.

"They're too impulsive. They might think they're being smart, but when they act on the spur of the moment they're forgetting an awful lot of things that can get them put away. They have no eye for detail", Ed stressed, pointin' to his own rheumy orb. A wild line of sweet talk, maybe, but it endeared him to Adeline. After all, Ed was a locally recognized authority on the subject, devourin' ev'ry detective magazine published.

Their first date was a weekend matinee at Plainfield's (only) picture palace. They sat speechless all the way through a Jimmy Stewart movie, Ed wolfin' copious amounts of popcorn. There's a pulse-racin' possibility they held hands, but no evidence they took their eyes from the screen. At the after-movie soda, Augusta was chief topic of conversation. Ed declared: "She was a saint. I've never met a woman who had anywhere near her amount of goodness. And I never expect to, either."

Adeline found this very sweet an' movin', but it made room for disagreement. On their next movie show date, she confessed she'd had a bellyful of her old widowed mother over the years, and, even though they shared a house together, she longed to move away. This was heresy in Ed's book. Realisin' there was no way he could put her straight, they parted as friends. End of courtship.

A few years later, when our boy had achieved a little fame, he was surprised to hear that Adeline had declared to a newspaper that he'd asked her to marry him. Flattered, by her comment that "I only turned him down because I didn't think I could live up to his expectations", but surprised all the same. Not even he foresaw the escalation of Death Row fan mail, when serial killers would become the new sex symbols. Nor could he predict a time when cranky dames like Adeline would write to Central State Hospital, beggin' for autographs, photos, even locks of his thinnin' hair. 'Other hand, it's likely he offended Adeline too, never invitin' her out to the Gein farmstead now he was all alone. But it wasn't the place it used to be.

Ed had no call to work the land anymore, and was sellin' it acre by acre. From 275, it was down to 160. No-one stepped foot in the place anymore, an' he didn't see the point of maintainin' its upkeep for ghosts. Once he'd sealed off Augusta's room in a state of perfect preservation, he made a kinda slob's resolution to let the house go all to hell too. He'd get home from makin' his meagre livin', rip open a can of soup or a jar of peanut butter, gulp the fodder down, no messin', an' think over what he was gonna do with his long, lonely evenin'.

Some nights, he'd get a kinda material nausea from noticin' the squalor all around him. All the tack an' garbage, all the stuff the Gein family never got to throw away. All our yesterdays: an old gas mask; used medicine bottles; old radios, still workin', though not much use in a house without electricity; a rusty horseshoe; a withered Christmas wreath. Add to this the debris of Ed's life - his cans, his discarded cereal packets, his discolored dentures, his collection of cereal box toys. Some nights, he'd need to get away from the whole festerin', twilit mess. He'd toss away his can, an' retire to his bedroom to read.

The garbage an' the darkness were encroachin' on his bedroom too, but they hadn't taken over. Yet.

Ilsa Koch: the She-Wolf of the S.S. Hmmm... int'resting young lady. Glad I never let Ma find these pictures. Some real racy stuff here, makes it all look kind of glamorous.

"After the end of the war, she was accused of keeping a collection of human heads and bodily parts. Most notoriously, she is known to have forced craftsmen among the death camp prisoners to make lampshades and bookbindings. Nothing too sinister about that - but the material used was THE SKIN OF THEIR FELLOW INMATES..."

Oh boy, what a doozy. Quite a dish, too. Truly terrible crimes, but imagine, just imagine, if you had a mind to let yourself off the leash...

"Among her more infamous crimes, the She-Wolf is also believed to have kept a collection of male sexual organs, preserved in

formaldehyde for her own evil gratification."
Oh dear Lord - why should I find a thing like that so amusing?
"Where's the pot of pickled pecker - Peter Piper's prick?" Damn,
but this stuff is int'resting.

Once the stories all dried up, there was still the loneliness.
Sometimes, out in the woods, tiny, twistin' branches could act as
friends. Arms stretchin' to the basement of Heaven, where Ma
now resided. But sometimes, even the bitin' night air couldn't
blow his darkness away.

One night, the sky was so red I knew it had been skinned, an'
those were its own flowing arteries. I kept list'ning for a voice -
my own, Ma's, the voice of God, anyone who would speak to me.
I heard nothing.

But I got a message through the nerve ends of my skin, tellin' me
to look behind. I looked up, an' saw the trees were bare and
dead - too naked even for that time of year. And from every
branch, there was a black-eyed, sleek-necked buzzard. Smilin' at
me. Gazin' down like I was easy prey. I felt I was one of Ma's
biblical prophets, pursued by demons... Or maybe like my Pa,
when he got sick with the DT's.

As an ex-farmer, Ed found his social standin' on a decline. He
knew some folks had always treated him as a clown, an oddity.
Now, he was beginnin' to wonder if he even had that status. The
land he had left was allotted out at $10 a year, a reasonable
peppercorn rent. A stream of small farmers came to sub-let - first
up, some of Elmo's boys, payin' in advance. But he'd been
neighborly enough to let five others pay their rent six months in
arrears. Bad mistake. He'd yet to see a penny, and one year on
Elmo's boys had made no further payment either. Sure, he kept
sweet-tempered, but all the while he knew he was bein'
snowjobbed.

When he felt a sense of injustice, he'd walk out to the cemetary
an' meditate at his mother's grave. The way you do, when y' need
to commune in your head with an absent loved one.

"Help me, Ma... give me the power to know when they're

deceivin' me. You know, you were right... I ain't got any clear of how to handle folks when you're not around."

When loneliness overwhelmed him, Ed got angry with himself. The words of longin' in his head were just a waste of time. His mother wasn't here - her soul was off wherever her Lord had taken her. Below the headstone that said **Augusta Gein - Beloved Mother** was an old bag of bones, a putrid corpse. It wasn't his Ma. So, deep inside of him, his demands got angrier.

Augusta Gein - I order you to rise from your idle bed. You've rested long enough. Wake up woman, I say! In the name of the Mother of God, and all that is holy, I call you once again... Awake, woman!

You just can't imagine all the concentration Ed put into his resurrection spell. Ever since the funeral, life had seemed a little unreal. He knew now, more than most, that what determines the world is the way you see it in your mind's eye. And he believed that maybe, if he thought long and hard enough, things might become a little more like the way he wanted them.

But Ma never came home. No matter how many nights he stood within the gates of that cemetary, his anger never overcame Death. Slowly, it occurred to Ed that he might be goin' about things the wrong way. The dark revelation was at hand.

In 1957, Edward Gein found himself under investigation for murder. During his interrogation by District Attorney Earl Kileen, the following exchange took place:

Q. "I have to ask you, Eddie, how many other women you recollect having killed."

A. "None, to my reckoning."

Q. (incredulous) "None?... No others? Come on, Eddie, the forensics boys estimate we could have remains from the bodies of up to 11 women at your place!"

A. "That could be true enough."

Q. "It sure could. So where have they all come from? Do you need a little time to drag up your memory?"

A. "Nope. Those women all came from the graveyard."

Q. "... They came from where?"

A. "The cemetary. They came from the cemetary. Hancock and Spritsfields sometimes, but mostly from Plainfield."

Q. "Are you trying to tell me that the female bodies you dismembered were all stolen from cemetaries?"

A. "That's about the size of it."

Q. "And that all the bodies looted from the graves were those of women? There were never any male, uh, victims?"

A. "Never any men. Wasn't interested."

Q. "Would you care to elaborate on these "activities"?"

A. (pause) "I guess I started to visit graveyards in the area regu'ly about 18 months after my mother died. Most nights I would just stand and have private conversations, quiet conversations, with my Ma, or the people I imagined were buried there. Other times, I couldn't make myself go home without raisin' one of 'em up first. Maybe on about nine occaisions, I took somebody, or part of somebody, home with me. It was kind of an evil spirit I couldn't control."

Q. "Jesus...
During what period did these desecrations take place?"

A. "Like I say, started about 18 months after Ma passed - 1947. Must have carried through to '52."

Q. "Five years?... And you never came under suspicion?"

A. "Don't see how I could have bin. I'd just open up the casket and take what I needed. Always left everything as it had been, in apple pie order."

Q. "Can you explain why you felt the compulsion to steal dead women from their graves?"

A. "After my mother died, I began to have strange visions. I developed an uncontrollable desire to see a woman's body. I began to visit cemetaries at night, when the moon was full... Had an aunt of mine worked in a lunatic asylum, told me once how patients went wild at this time of month. One night, I dug up the body of a woman who had just been

43

buried. I took it home. It gave me a great deal of satisfaction... Then I began to watch the papers for obituaries of women. The night after they were buried, I would go to the cemetary and open up their graves."

The first time... ever Ed saw her face... She was puce green an' fadin' fast. The color of decay, an' the rain-fed burial ground. He'd worked hard, with no sense of panic , knowin' there was no night watchman to disturb (who the Sam Hill would wanna steal

anythin' from a burial ground?). The shovel sifted through the wet earth like an expectant bridegroom, hungry for the promise of tender bliss. Breathin' heavy, Ed hauled the smooth new casket out, hardly believin' his own gumption. Hardly believin' his own madness. In the discolored face 'a that handsome, matronly woman, he glimpsed a universal motherhood. This was the way they all became, once they went beneath the soil. All good women, all the mothers of Jesus, were one in death.

After the first time, Ed always saw Augusta in those peaceful, rotten faces. Her grave was sacred - but there were plenty other flowers of the boneyard to pick. Soon, he learned how to dif'rentiate between his ladies. The trick was too look beyond her face, to the other body parts.

I had the top part of her casket caved in... Shoddy craftsmanship, truly a sin... Seemed I had a straight choice. Take her out bit by bit, the hole in that crumblin' damp wood not big enough to let her out in toto. Otherwise, I could take just take out what I wanted. Pickin' her out in pieces would've been very difficult - I admit it to myself, though I'd find it hard to confess to others. Like to think, if things had been dif'rent, I coulda been a medical man - darn sure I was as skillful as a good vet'rinarian - but just then it was beyond my capability. So I went to my toolbox... Worked my way through the stringy throat meat an' the gristle of her trachea, just like Ma would carve a joint of mutton. Hit bone in no time flat. Never brought a saw, so I had to work her head one way... then the other... back... an' it fought like loose chicken wire... an' forth... where I could feel the elastic top of the spine bendin' before it broke. All of a sudden, her dusty hair flopped into my hands, she reclinin' like some sad broken ragdoll. She was mine. I looked at her. Shut-eye, peaceful repose, only the broken peak of her vertebral column pokin' out her raw neck disturbed her serenity. Not ashamed to admit it now - I was overjoyed. Felt like kissin' her right there on the mouth. But I guess I was a little shy...

Thought about leavin' right then, but I had unfinished business. Was it right to take from her what I'd never tried to take from a woman before? Now, I can't be too clear on it either way. But back then, I had it straight. I talked to Ma about it, in my head - she told me that once a woman left this life, she'd be spared of all the burden her sex lays on her. So I was blameless. What I took from her wasn't hers anymore. It belonged to me an' God, an' no-one else.

I broke through the bottom half of that casket, an' worked with all the delicacy I could muster.

Chapter Four
THE TRANSFORMATION OF EDWARD GEIN

"God may be nearer to Mr. Gein than the rest of us, because God comes closer to people in dealings with life and death. Mr. Gein is closer to such things than the rest of us."
THE REVERAND KENNETH ENGLEMAN
FORMER METHODIST PASTOR
OF WAUTOMA, WISCONSIN

Grown-up innocents like Ed never truly leave youth behind. As the years rolled into the early 1950's, a time of apple pie, ice cream an' the A-bomb, he became more of a social animal than you might think possible. Drug stores, news stands, taverns, you never knew where that quaint little guy was gonna walk in an' treat you to the benefit of his wisdom. Most folks knew his repertoire by now - murder cases, the customs of primitive societies... an' women.

That's right. Our bashful little guy had reached a stage where he could talk about the fair sex without blushin' like a stop light. True, he'd needed the safe distance of middle age before he could broach the subject. If he ever acted lecherous, it was on account of dames his own age - way out of the bobbysoxer stakes. But, like most guys, it was just a playful tease. No harm meant. Never any harm in ol' Ed.

But the only folks that got close enough to penetrate his shell of loneliness were young people. I mean real young people - kids. Billy Hill, son of Lester and Irene, could be said to've bin one of the few regular buddies Ed had. Young Bill was knockin' on his teens. This was still an age, remember, when "early teenager" meant little boy or girl, nothin' more. Nat'rally, Bill's preoccupations were still very much those of a kid. Climbin' trees, model airplanes, war movies. These were int'rests an eternal adolescent like Ed could share. Many's the time they would attend the attend the Saturday matinees, watchin' Audie Murphy win that far-off war.

Was only a matter of time before Billy saw fit to invite himself to the rundown ol' Gein farmhouse. By now, it loomed large in the imagination of ev'ry kid in Plainfield. Dank with gloom an' disrepair, even the smallest of 'em knew it was haunted.

"Hiya, Eddie... this is my pal, Jim. Okay if we come in an' see those Fokker bi-planes you told me about?"

Ed gave his meek, slope-eyed smile, an' opened the door. Hospitality came surprisinly nat'ral, considerin' no-one else had walked through that unlit portal for nearly a ten-year. Jim couldn't help rollin' his eyes around the unlit squalor, the way gawky, gawping kids are wont to do.

"If this place ain't haunted, I sure bet it's infested", he whispered in Billy's ear.

"Clam up, jackass, he'll hear you!", the boy chuckled, punchin' his friend's arm. He knew that, if Ed heard, he probably wouldn't care anyway. Ed was just about the funniest, most easy-goin' grown-up he'd met. In that sense, he was no grown-up at all.

"Step your way around the junk, fellers... I'll get round to cleaning this place some day soon." Under their astonished view, even Ed had to become conscious of the pigsty he lived in. There was no way his visitors could step around anythin'. Ev'ry step wobbled on a can, or squashed somethin' rotten. It was only from the dirty, sepia light of the living room window they could pick out an occaisional object.

"You play all these things, Eddie?" Billy pointed to the musical instruments lying around in disarray.

"Oh, after a fashion", Ed grinned modestly. "Learned a little light classical, little polka, little hootenanny. Nothin' much the young people would know."

The violin leaned 'gainst the armchair had only two strings left. An' the piano accordian had its squeezebox broken. Broken relics of a broken life.

"You two take yourselves a drink." Ed doled out lemonade he'd squeezed 'specially for the occaision, in chipped china cups. "I'll

be rummagin' through my collection... Won't take long, but I
have to keep my eyes real sharp", he nodded toward a black hole
down the corridor. "Never found the time to get those 'lectric
lights installed."

The kids looked at each other, chuckled some more. Who'd
believe they'd found someone downright odd enough to live like
this? But then, a small town could only hold one of ol' Ed. Billy
kinda liked the novelty of it.

"Hey, I bet Eddie's got enough trash in here to keep the garbage
collectors busy now 'til doomsday!"

"Yeah", grimaced lanky Jim, wrinklin' his nose at the heavy
odors in the air. "I'm wonderin' how he ain't permanent sick!"
Billy read the unease on his face, an' started to poke fun. "What
ya say we take a peek inside his bedroom, find out how much
garbage he's storing in there?"

"Go take a hike! Why, he's... he's liable to get angry!"

"Angry? Ed? Nawww, he's the least angriest grown-up there is.
C'mon, let's take ourselves a tour."

They didn't even make it as far as the bedroom. Ed's door was
held fast open by a heap 'a debris. Jim's attention was grabbed by
somethin' hangin' from an unevenly-planed wall cupboard.

"Hey... will your get your eyes on this!" His nervousness got
flushed away in a rush of morbid excitement. He unhooked a
cord from a coat hanger, wavin' the ornament in Billy's face. A
leathery, shrivelled head, skin the color of mildly charred paper.
"Yup... she's a shrunken head alright. Genuine native handi-
work." The boy dropped the leathery dome when he heard Ed's
liltin' voice. It thudded 'gainst the door. Two low-hangin' sisters
came to light, ker-knockin' their dead skulls 'gainst each other.

"Shr... shrunken heads?", asked Billy, his heartbeat comin' back
down to normal. "Like in the jungle pictures?"

"That's right", said Ed, not riled by their adventurin'. He picked
up the head, lookin' with admiration at her sewn-shut eye sockets.
"The Fillipino tribes open up the skull... take out the eyes, the
brain, an' part of the skull. Then they bake it in their own tradi-

49

tional herbs an' spices, Colonel Sanders-style. By the time the skin tightens, you got your very own nat'ral Jack O' Lantern. Ain't she pretty?" Ed held up her sister for contrast. She had distended, fleshy lips, like they were puckered out artificially with nails.

"You mean, that thing's from a real person?" Jimmy was turnin' green. "The skin felt more like a, like a..."

"Like a gnarled old cowhide? That's the effect of the process. My cousin Clem from La Crosse told me all about it - picked these up in a Manilla street market durin' the last war world war." Billy handled the stitched heads with renewed int'rest. "Will ya look at that?... genuine shrunken heads. Wait 'til I tell ev'ryone at school."

Jim couldn't raise the same enthusiasm. "They don't look so shrunk to me", he muttered, mostly to himself. "... More like regular size." It spoiled the whole visit for Jim. Didn't do much more than nod with disint'rest when Ed took out his fighter plane collection. When they left, he swore to Bill he wasn't ever steppin' in that madhouse again. Not ever. Billy joshed him for bein' nervy, but he never found the spunk to pay Ed a visit after that. From that day forth, Ed had one more livin' visitor to his property as long as he resided there.

The loneliness was still under his skin. After the boys left for home, he took himself walkin' in the woods, tryin' to shake the mood. Lately, life was more like a dream than reality. Even when he was around other people, it just didn't feel like he could connect with much anymore.

The autumnal woods gave a smell of burnin' foliage, of waste an' regret, but its source seemed far, far away. Ed knew there were no neighbors near enough to prick his nose with a burnin' leaf pile. It was just his sense playin' tricks on him. They did that a lot lately.

He trudged through a yellowin' mound of pine an' oak leaves. Didn't have the spirit to kick 'em, just tramped in up to his knees.

If he stared for just one moment, their serrated edges made the outline of a face, their lined markin's were grotesque features. Just like anyone else with half an imagination. If he stared for longer, they took on the familiar features of decay. But not the peaceful, saggy flesh masks he'd learned to share his life with. These were movin'. Mockin'. Eyeless, but starin'. If he didn't force his attention elsewhere, he'd hear 'em mutter an' shriek. As he turned tail for the farm, he could hear the dead laugh at him. Laughin' at Edward T. Gein, stranded in the world of the livin', where he didn't belong.

He wasn't safe on his own anymore, not unless he was back at the farmhouse. In the refuge of his own imagination. The darkness was movin' in, faster an' faster.

ON DECEMBER 9, 1954, TAVERN OWNER MARY HOGAN, AGED 54, OF PINE GROVE, WISCONSIN, DIS-APPEARED. SHE WAS NEVER SEEN ALIVE AGAIN. ON NOVEMBER 16, 1957, EDWARD GEIN'S FARM-HOUSE WAS ENTERED BY LAW OFFICERS FROM ALL OVER WAUSHARA COUNTY, IN CONNECTION WITH THE DISAPPEARANCE OF ANOTHER WOMAN. THEY WERE LATER JOINED BY THE PINE GROVE POLICE, STILL BAFFLED BY THE CASE OF MARY HOGAN.

In the sanity hearings which formed a large proportion of the eventual trial of Ed Gein, a social worker from Central State Hospital put together his personal assessment of the defend-ant. He was described as suffering from confusion, and apparent occaisional loss of memory. He was also described as contented, and at ease with hospital staff. He viewed their professional approach as a form of acceptance, something he claimed not to have experienced in his home community for many years. During his initial period at Central State, he underwent a thorough series of medical examinations. The doctor who observed the state of Gein's health commented thus:

"The patient seemed in generally good health, despite a mild disturbance in vision by a growth over the left eye. The only recurring problems experienced were of a purely psychological nature. Under examination, he complained of headaches, nausea, and bad odors, which appeared to be purely psychosomatic. During the course of an examination, he broke down without warning, and started whimpering, very much in the manner of a child. When asked what caused his distress, he complained of symptoms which seemed to have no origin in his physical condition. He complained that he smelled something unpleasant, which was making him grow nauseous. "It's a crazy smell", was all he could say. When prompted further, he elaborated that "it smells like flesh. It smells like the grave." By this time, the patient was in tears."

A lonely man drinks his time away. Any country 'n' western singer'll tell you that. Ed was no dif'rent, though he was not gonna rival Hank Williams for conspicuous consumption. He'd just kinda sit on that stool, drinkin' in more of what folks around him were sayin' than he would of his own brew.

"Any of you boys ever thought about changin' your sex?", he asked one night.

"Say what, Ed?" The whole bar went as quiet as a western saloon when the white-hat stranger walks in.

"I've been reading a real int'resting story in the papers. Seems this G.I. has left the army and gone to Denmark. They've developed this operation whereby a feller can change his sex. If he'd be more happy with bein' a woman, that is."

This was surely some serious strangeness. The barman spoke up on behalf of the whole assembly. "How in hell can a guy change his sex? That can't be possible, not to man nor beast."

Ed nodded, acceptin' their plain ignorance. "It can be done all right. The doctors can do it. I suppose if a guy studied the right books, he could do it all himself. I've been thinking about it a lot."

A moment's silence, an' the whole bar burst into laughter. Weird ol' Ed - never can take him too serious.

Now, this place where he was drinkin' was out in Pine Grove, 'bout four miles from Plainfield, six miles from the farmstead. It didn't seem none too practical to drink this far from home, but Ed had gotten fascinated with the environment. More particu'ly, he'd got acquainted with Mary, the manageress of the tavern.

She was a friendly, backslappin' figure - not just with Ed, but with all the guys in the bar. "Hiya, sleepytime Joe, howya doin'?", she'd ask, ribbin' him for his half-awake look. Ed didn't mind. She treated ev'ryone the same way - in fact she was more like a goodnatured guy than any woman he'd met before. That fascinated Ed. He had gender, an' the attendant problems thereof, on his mind a whole lot in those days. How much happier would they all be, he wondered, if Mary had been born just a regular guy, an' he could take her place as a woman? It bore thinkin' about, but it sure was a problem.

"Here, have a hit of bourbon on me, you deerstalkin' guy, you!" She'd get a little soused an' pull the cap down over his eyes. Took him for a hunter, not knowin' how squeamish he could get about the sight of a slaughtered beast. Ed didn't mind. He'd always turn the bourbon down, account of how he'd had to drive over, an' never havin' touched a drop of the evil spirit anyway... It was around this time he decided he liked Mary. Liked her, but had a small problem with her attitude. In all of Ed's experience, there were two kinds 'a women. There was the personable, motherly type, the woman he'd grown up to respect. Then there was the flirty, painted Jezebel - all blown up an' blowsy on ac- count 'a her prettiness, an' milkin' it for what it was worth. Ed was a liberal type of guy - he'd lightened up his views over the years, not thinkin' of this kinda woman much worse than his Ma did of the sluttish mothers of Plainfield.

But a feller had to have standards. Where Mary fitted into it, he didn't know. She was not one nor the other, an' Ed no longer had the maternal guidance he needed to pigeonhole her. It bothered

Ed a lot.

It still bothered him when he went over to the Hills to run a few errands next day, account of Irene's assistant clerk in the grocery store bein' sick.

She was runnin' off the order of Ed's deliveries, when he got himself fascinated by the twinklin' of a butcher's blade.

"... Now this box of cabbages and miniature pork chops has to go over to Mrs. Beckley. She's gettin' harder of hearin' at her time of life, so Scottie normally gets her attention by throwin' stones at the dog and gettin' him to bark. You make sure that she pays on delivery, 'cos... Ed? Are you listening to me, dear?"

He would have if he could. Right now, her reflection in the blade was hypnotizin' him.

"Lordsakes, Ed, you'll cut yourself with that darned thing!"

She was right enough. He'd got so far into his thoughts, the prick of the knife in his finger registered itself, but not the pain as it drew blood. He smiled his helpless smile, an' all was forgiven. Mighty big woman like Irene, she could never expect danger from a shrimp like Ed. She was a robust, hearty woman - like Ma was, but without the holy fervour. Like Mary was, but without the smell of whiskey.

Ed still couldn't hear her as she talked. Seein' her glisten in the blade had given him ideas. Not ideas he recognised in his logical mind, but instinctive ideas that rose up as feelin's.

In the sanity hearing of 1974, Dr. Thomas Malueg of Central State Hospital, Wisconsin, testified to Judge Gollmar as to Ed Gein's mental condition. He agreed with the patient that his "thought processes were now generally intact and reasonably well organised." However, he stressed that he would become angry whenever asked about his crimes:

"I don't want to rake up the past. If you stir up the past, you might get burned up in your own fire. I figure psychiatrists are responsible for a lot of trouble in the world, account of people diggin' up the past. A lot of the prisoners from here

might go out an' kill 'em, rob 'em, club 'em... all because of digging up the past!"
Malueg tried Ed with his personal interpretation of a few well-worn cliches. His most individual response was to "a bird in the hand is worth two in the bush":
"If you have a bird in your hand, you might squeeze him too much and kill him."

At Mary Hogan's bar, Ed took to listenin' to local gossip, somethin' a Christian soul was rarely inclined to do. "That Mary", a friendly, sozzled barstool buff leaned over an' told him, "...she's lived more life than any man or woman I know in the whole county!" Ed smiled an' winked his barely open eye, though he was none too sure what the guy meant. But if you held your tongue an' listened, you could learn a whole lot. Seemed Mary had travelled a little - as far abroad as the state of Illinois - an' had gotten involved in some ventures that were not as above board as the tavern.
"Place where a man can enjoy the company of women, without too much fuss as to takin' her home or buyin' her gifts. A bawdy institution, if you take my drift."
So that was it. There was sin in her, after all. Ed had sensed it intutively, but now he had confirmation. Oh, it mighta been hearsay, but there was no smoke without fire. It was somethin' he still had to reconcile.
I liked her. I realised I liked her a whole lot. I liked her so much I knew I'd have to kill her.
"An' how you doin' tonight my lit'le honey?" Mary leaned her big, homely face over the bar, showin' off her fleshy jowls.
"Bin worse, Mary. Bin a whole lot worse", he winked without much effort. "Say, Mary... I've had a little something on my mind", our boy said conspiratorially, with the confidence that had taken 48 years to hatch.
"Oh yeah? And you wanna tell me what that something is?", she smiled at him, blowin' cigarette smoke from her fat face.

"Well... I'd like you to go ice skating with me, Mary."
She raised a pencilled eyebrow. Ed was serious. He was an odd
one, but at her age you learned to catch as catch can. "Ahh, well
ain't you sweet? You know I'd love to, Eddie, but I can't skate."
She tweaked his chin, far less fleshy than her own.
"That's okay, neither can I. I figured we could hold onto each
other 'stead of falling down flat." It was the neatest come-on Ed
could fabricate, and it'd serve him well more than once.
Mary laughed, feelin' nervously flattered. She'd never truly
figured little Eddie as the type, but he seemed to mean it. The
night wore on, an' she shifted her buxom frame from behind the
bar to where Ed was sittin'.
"So what do you do with yourself, Eddie... Out there in the
woodlands, all alone at night?"
He felt like she was teasin', but that was okay. In his way, he was
teasin' too.
"Oh, I have things to do. Hobbies."
"What kinda hobbies?", she squinted all suspicious, believin' his
reticence to be a put-on. "I bet you're a huntin' man. Got a barn
full of stagheads. Am I right?"
"Uh-uh. That's not me. I carve a keen joint of venison now an'
then, but I'm no hunter."
"I know just what you mean, Ed. Too much of a gamey smell
around the place."
"We-ell", he considered. "Not really that. I'm somethin' of an
expert on embalming. Dead animals wouldn't bother my nose so
much."
Mary was fascinated. For rural Wisconsin, Ed was a Renaissance
man. Not only an expert criminologist, but a craftsman to boot.
She stayed enrapt to Ed, listenin' all night to his specialised
subjects. None of the other customers paid much heed - only a
few of 'em in the place anyway - account of the way she still
went wheezin' up an' down the bar, makin' sure ev'ryone got
their customary talkin' to. The end of the night, Ed received a
request he never thought he'd hear from a woman at his time

oflife.

"You have many lady visitors back at your farmhouse, Eddie?" Ed replied that, in truth, he hadn't entertained a livin' soul in quite some time. Mary reflected on how she was lonely too, how nice it would be to share a nightcap with a friend, before retirin' on this cold an' lonely night.

"Yup", replied Ed, "that would be nice. The night don't hold any fears when you're with a friend."

Come midnight, Mary was shuttin' off the taps an' boltin' the doors. Her new boyfriend was waitin' with the collar on his checked wincheated turned up. "Comin', comin', comin' right up!", she sang, bobbin' along like a cheerleader with a drink problem.

"Say, Mary", said Ed, as she pinched his high cheekbone. "Did you remember to close all the windows?"

"Why... sure, Ed", she said as she tugged on her mackintosh.

"How about the blinds? You pull those down too?"

"Those as well. What in the world is worryin' you, Eddie?" She smiled at him, taken by how shy he was comin' on at this late stage.

"Oh, I'm not worried, Mary. There's just too many folks around who don't mind pryin' on a body, that's all."

"Oh, don't have a mind about them. Get your car key now, sweetness, Mary's ready to go!"

"I'm glad of that, Mary. I'm real glad."

Ed took Henry's old .22 pistol from his pocket. He aimed it at her without droppin' the dumb smile from his face.

"Why, Ed... what kind of crazy game are you playin' now?" He was surely the wackiest guy she'd ever hooked up with - but he was fun, in his own weird way.

"Shut your eyes, Mary. I got a surprise for you."

She screwed up her tipsy eyes, pursin' out her full pink lips like she was ready to play Postman's Knock.

Ed gave her a knockout kiss from the barrel of his gun. Shot her just above the bridge of the nose, dentin' the bottom of her forehead. Mary lost the smile, but otherwise hit the floor like she'd sat down without a barstool.

Ed took her wet table rag from the sink below the bar. Wiped up the stains from the floor, screwin' up soft brain, splintered cranium bone an' mops of blood in the palm of his hand, then squashed up the rag, foldin' it in his pocket.

"Hot damn..." He had one hell of task in front of him. Glad that he'd had a fine example for good, Christian hard work, he hoisted Mary's consid'rable body by her upturned legs, draggin' her out of the bar to his pick-up. Only human trace left of Mary was a wet pink trail leakin' from the back of her head, mixin' with the soapy water on the floor...

D.A. KILEEN: "Were you only interested in female corpses because of some, uh, sexual obsession?"
GEIN (a little offended): "No, sir. I wasn't."
KILEEN: "Did you at any time procure a dead female for the purpose of sexual intercourse?"
GEIN: "No sir, I did not... They smelled too bad."
KILEEN: "Then what would you say your motivation was in seeking out deceased females?"
GEIN: "The hair. Longer hair seemed of more value to me. Needed it for my raw materials."

Ed was back to farm laborin', though he no longer tended his own sterile ground. Elmo Ueeck an' him were munchin' through their vittles, exchangin' unwanted small talk the way Ed was always doin' of late.

"This Mary Hogan thing...", Ed contemplated between mouthfuls, "I reckon she was tied up with some bad people, that's how she disappeared."

"So I've heard some say. But that's just idle talk. People can make all the guesses they want." Elmo screwed up his lean eagle face, unimpressed.

"Oh, she was into somethin' bad alright. I heard folks say she was tied up in some crooked business... An' I tell you what else I know."

"What?", Elmo enquired, knowin' Ed would tell him whether he wanted to hear or not.

"The police are messin' this whole thing up. The guy who did away with poor Mary won't be caught."

"I thought it was always the criminal who blundered, in your book."

"Only when he gets caught. I guess this guy's not going to be. This time, the police are making the mistakes."

Elmo rounded on the amateur detective with a wry ol' buzzard smile. "How do you know she's been killed?"

"Well...", Ed hesitated. "She hasn't been kidnapped, because there's been no ransom note. Oh, she's been killed all right. The guy shot her. Then dragged her into the woods an' buried her. Hell, there's a million acres of woods in this country! They'll never find her!"

Elmo nodded, packin' his canteen away. Ed was onto his fav'rite subject, but it just didn't have the same appeal for him.

"Yup, sure is a shame about her."

"Sure is."

"She was some woman. Kinda like Frank Worden's ma - you know her?"

"Bernice? We're a little acquainted."

"Sure, Bernice. She's nice an' plump. A real woman, just like Mary."

Elmo remembered him as rollin' his eyes an' wigglin' his nose at this point, like a dog sniffin' a skunk.

"Wanna know somethin'?... Mary's not missin'. I got her hung up back at my place right now!"

Elmo looked at Ed behavin' like a wild-eyed coot. "Let's get back to work. You're always talkin' crazy these days!" He just didn't see the funny side.

As time ticked on, Ed found that even his hobbies couldn't

holdaway the loneliness. He was livin' more an' more in his head these days, not frequentin' the taverns so much since Mary went missin'. One cold an' dewy April day, he resolved to change his life for good.

Jane Hartman was a quiet country housewife, pretty, on the skinny side, not long wed. Her an' her husband lived in a small cottage next door to the Hills' place. They didn't have any land of their own to run a farm, so John Hartman was out workin' when Ed came to call. Jane was surprised to see him, but not alarmed. After all, Ed was known as a semi-hermit these days, a harmless eccentric. And he sometimes ate his meals over at the Hills', so he wasn't exactly a stranger.

"Got a business proposition for ya", said Ed, respectfully doffin' his cap. She handed him a cup of coffee an' waited bemusedly for the details. Ev'ryone knew Ed was a little slow-witted. What could he possibly have to offer them?

"It's the ol' house. Just seems like I don't need all that space any more, me a confirmed bachelor an' all. Wonderin' whether you an' your husband might consider exchangin' homes?"

She was cautious, but more than a little tempted. Her an' John were plannin' to start a family, an' their modest little place would be more than enough to provide. But still... nine rooms, Eddie Gein said he had at the farmhouse. That would be a grand start in life for any little Johns or Janes.

On checkin' the place out, Mrs. Hartman soon realised who'd be gettin' the raw end of the deal. "Could... could you please open a window?", she pleaded, almost gaggin'. Ed rolled the dirty, opaque frame up along its rail. She couldn't hold the pretence of politeness, holdin' her pointed little nose for all she was worth. The garbage on the floor had long taken pride of place, though it was too dark to identify any of it. An' too ever-present not to go squelchin' your way through.

Ed tutted. "Look how I been neglecting my household duties... Let's go through the kitchen, Miss, have ourselves a little lemon-ade." He ushered her through, she holdin' off the stench with a handkerchief. She hoped to find relief from the foul air. But, as he entered the jumbled mess of dirty pots, fryin' pans an' cereal packets, her flat walkin' shoes took a ride. Just about caught herself, holdin' herself from goin' belly down with the palm of her hands. "What... what is this?", she asked Ed as he helped her to her feet, him so apologetic. Her light blue dress was slimy with pungent grease, her hands stank of it too.

"I guess that's meat fat", admitted Ed, feelin' a little foolish. "Musta spilled it on the floor sometime."

The kitchen floor was like an ice rink in a butcher's store. Ev'ry spot was smeared with the grease, or with some foul stain. She never let got of Ed's bashful grasp. Her stomach was so unsettled, she thought she'd just keel right over. She finally supported herself over the sink, the fossilised mesh of ancient cutlery holdin' her from pukin' straight into the bowl. She felt somethin' soft down at the sole of her shoe. Rat. Dirty, great brown rat. Dead rat. Nicely divided down the middle by a shot from Ed's .22.

All she could do was laugh. Somehow, it was in the keepin' with the decor of the place. Out of the corner of her eye, she saw three glass apothecary jars, holdin' somethin' dark grey. Large grey balls with deep curves, like... human brains?

"That there is chewing gum. After I chew it a day or so, I roll it up an' store it in the jar. That way, I get to use it again. Some of that gum is over five years old."

She nodded approval of her thriftiness, but all she wanted was out. Unnerved, she saw a back door leadin' off the kitchen, an' tried to make light. "Is that where you keep your shrunken heads, Mr. Gein?", she alluded to the legend of his ornaments. "Oh no", he answered, pointin' plain serious out to the hall, "I got 'em in a cupboard out there."

Not even Ed's offer of a joint of venison to take home could hold her one moment longer. Ed put it all down to her bein' a shy young woman, an' waited for her husband's response in hope. Sad to tell, it never came. Ed was stuck in his dark house of dreams, at least for the forseeable future.

On November 16 of that fateful year, more officers of the law
than could fill a police convention converged on the Gein
place. Ed was locked up safely out of the way, so they had to
let their noses, and their bewildered instincts, be their guide.
They were like some monastic brotherhood in a vow of collec-
tive silence. Ev'rywhere they shone their torchlights, a face
stared back. With no anger, no curiosity. Just the blank
serenity of death.
"What in hell?...", snarled newly elected sheriff Arthur
Schley. Just a few months on from givin' warnings for traffic
violations - now he had the interior of Hell starin' at him, in
the guise of a rundown ol' junk heap.
"... Some kinda... mask... or somethin'." He held the baggy,
pouchy, female features at arm's length. It looked realistic
enough, apart from the greyin', witchy-poo hair. But it had
nothin' but wide-open cuts where an eyesocket should be, and
the jawline was wild, torn, asymmetrical...
"It's a kind of mask alright", a bespectacled guy from
Waushara's forensics squad answered slowly, drinkin' in the
evidence of his own eyes. But that's no synthetic material, or
any animal hide. Only thing I've seen that starts to discolor
like these is human flesh."
The collected murmurs of outrage didn't seem to form coher-
ent words. They peeled 'em off walls, out of cupboards, out
of discarded refuse sacks. They counted nine so far. No-one
said it, but they all had to silently face up. Little Ed Gein
had been makin' Hallow'een costumes out of real live women.
And such a craftsman... Some of 'em were dried out, mummified, almost lackin' in features. They must've been the
early efforts, for he'd surely acquired some skill since startin'
out. On the end of wooden poles, the lawmen held out stolen
human faces that appeared to be younger than their sisters.
At least, they'd stopped agin'. Soft an' feminine, they were

preserved somehow, the skins soaked in some gentle oil to hold 'em from decay.Labours of love. Some even had lipstick, smeared on with less precision than the skillful peelin' of the faces. Ed wanted his ladies to look like ladies. Four were stuffed out with old newspaper to make 'em rich an' fulsome. Split lips almost smilin', in the full bloom of health. "Over here", shouted one of the deputies, angry with himself that he should be the one to find it. From a brown paper bag he produced a fleshy, female face, some of the fatty tissue still attached to the skin. "Hellfire an' shit...", he whispered, "it's Mary Hogan." For those who'd know these women, it wouldn't be so hard to identify their faces.

By the time reporters from all over the country had descended on tiny Plainfield, the law enforcers had their own personal theories. The director of the Central State crime laboratory of Wisconsin believed that most of the masks would be found to contain formaldehyde - "Our noses tell us."

"So the presence of embalming fluid supports the suspect's defence, that he's merely a graverobber?", asked a radio reporter. He looked around to his colleagues for support, found only bemusement. "Maybe he's an amateur taxidermist."

Thus did a moment's conjecture turn into a popular myth. Meanwhile, the sheriff from nearby Portage County was positive they had mass murder on their hands. "Yeah, there are strong traces of formaldehyde, but they're on the Hogan woman's death mask too, an' we know he killed her. Ed Gein never robbed a grave in his life."

The Portage County Sheriff, D.A. Kileen, and the sexton of Plainfield Cemetary all contended it was just plain impossible for Ed to have taken bodies from the ground. Most bodies were buried beneath heavy headstones. How in hell could 140-pound Ed pull that off by himself?

There was an uproar in the small town. It was just about

divided 'tween those who felt they had to know whether their loved ones had been resurrected an'violated, an' those who would rather it be that Ed had massacred many missin', half-forgotten women from all around the area. In the end, somethin' had to give. Sheriff Schley, a tall, stocky young man, bullied a short list of the abused dead out of Ed 'fore he went for his psychiatric examination. Some guy from the Plainfield town board, name of Wing, insisted that a couple of the named graves should be opened, to allay the public's fear. His sister-in-law, a Mrs. Eleanor Adams, had been buried in Plainfield six years previous, right next to Augusta Gein. She was on Ed's list, so up she had t' come. The townsfolk were just too unnerved by Ed's unlikely soundin' statements. Sometimes, he said, he would return to the graves an' put back the skeletons, the pieces he didn't want. When the investigatin' team went to the grave, it took the sexton an' his assistant just one hour to disinter the coffin of Eleanor Adams. The casked had been placed within a much larger wooden box, beginnin' two feet underground. When the grave was freshly dug, a dilligent, hard-workin' soul like Ed would have made short work of it.

I had her lyin' there - weren't another option for my poor soul to take. Besides... it wasn't like she was a genuine woman. Hell no. Mrs. Adams had upped an' gone to her maker these last five days. Whatever else I may have done, I didn't break any command- ments. Not even the one about adultery. Mrs. Adams weren't no married woman any more. She was just... a sack of life that was dryin' up. I could strip away her white dress. Cut through the corset that was workin' its way into her skin - all stuck tight, like a soaked wet sackcloth.

But she was dryer than any human being I'd come across. Up 'til then, that is. I felt my way around the area my books called "mons veneris". That was Latin for what Ma used to call each woman's personal cross. She believed it was the gateway to sin, and I've heard some fellers tell like it's a short cut to heaven. Not to me. Just seemed like a beaver left in a trap for too long. Such a cold, crazy feeling, with those soft-lookin' hairs scratchin' me like a wirebrush. Was starting to smell a little gamey too, like dead critters do. But I didn't fuss any. It was the start of my trueeducation.

First, I parted the outer labia with my jacknife... kinda like the drawbridge to the gateway itself. Hardly seems real to me now. It all looked scary, but it opened up so fresh an' soft. Like a great flower blooming, right there in the sunbeam glow of my torch-lamp. Everything I'd read about was true. The gateway opened wide, and I beheld the glory of womankind.

All the soft tissue cut away real easy, but I tried not to make her a mess. Everything flushed red, but she never really bled. Guess Mrs. Adams had been too long at peace.

Sometimes it was like fileting a live salmon, that didn't have the sense to stop squirimin' an die. But soon enough it all came good. I could reach in with both hands and pull the whole precious load away, without stringin' on too many loose tissues. Once I'd finished, I scooped up her spillage in a bowl, for the garbage heap. Seems such a crazy thing to me now. I wrapped Mrs. Adams up in an old blanket, like I wanted her to keep warm 'til I came back to explore some more. Guess I just wanted to show a little respect.

KILEEN: "Mary Hogan..."
GEIN: "I liked Mary, she reminded me of my mother somehow."
KILEEN: "You killed her, Ed, all the same. What did you do to her body when you got it home?"
GEIN: "I strung her up in the summer kitchen. The shed my father built for slaughtering pigs. I cut her up. I saved some of the parts and burned those I didn't want."
KILEEN: "Did you keep her genital organs?"
GEIN: "I don't rightly remember."
KILEEN: "Do you have any recollection of taking any fe-

male body parts - the vagina, specifically - and holding it over your penis to cover the penis?"

GEIN: "I believe that's true."

KILEEN: "Would you ever put on a pair of women's panties over your body, and then put some of these vaginas over your penis?"

GEIN: "That could be."

KILEEN: "Have you ever used the facial skins you took as masks, placing them over your own face?"

GEIN: "That I did."

KILEEN: "... And would you wear those faces over a prolonged time?"

GEIN: "Not too long. I used to have other things to do."

On those milder moonlit nights, Ed used to get dressed up like a dog's dinner. The little guy had talents, no-one can take that away from him. Amateur surgeon. Embalmer. Hunter of humans. An' a darn nifty tailor too...

He'd treated an' primed his fabrics, 'til they were fit to last as long as a human lifetime. Matter 'a fact, they outlived the women they were taken from in the first place.

He stood out on a hill, all dressed up an' nowhere to go. Naked except for his own skin, an' the skin of sev'ral others.

Had the sexiest pair of leg stockings - two solid flanks of flesh, tied tightly with nylon thread to his own. Strapped on an upper coat of skin, an' tied the cords hard 'til the upper torso was his own. A patchwork of beauty. The abdomen of a woman had been tanned an' hardened, 'til it could transform the wearer himself. Under the glarin' mother moon, Ed became the object of his own desires. The moon set him free, the coat of arms made him someone else. He banged with a jawbone on his gut-skinned drum, havin' the time of his life.

No longer trapped by nature, he could howl out to his own god, the Mother God, to make him become the woman of his own dreams. Once, he would've prayed to God, other times he'd talk to Ma - but now he was his own salvation. With a pair of saggin', jelly-filled tits tied around him, he was reborn a goddess. With all his inhibitions gone, he howled to the moon, wild an' pagan. Ma would never have approved, but now he was holy. Now, he called out to her through the soft pit of feminity he had attached to his face. Her God-fearin' little boy had made a blood sacrifice.

Ed Gein, at the time of his arrest

Chapter Five
THE DEER HUNT

**"Edward Gein is one of the most dramatic
human beings ever to confront society" -
one of numerous psychiatric opinions
given at the time of the Gein hearings.**

The huntin' season was gonna be a good one. Most of the
men in Waushara County, an' a good many 'a the women, had
their weapons polished an' ready for the weigh-in. Even Ed, the
guy who couldn't stand the sight of a a slaughtered full-grown
animal, felt the optimism an' electricity in the air.
He whistled to himself as he drove into Plainfield on the eve of
the hunt, Friday the 15th of November. Waved to Bernard
Muschinksy, owner of Plainfield's gas station, settin' up scales on
his forecourt for the weighin' of the deer. Havin' parked up his
old Ford sedan, he stepped into the Worden hardware store.
"Evenin' Bernice... Frank", Ed called in his friendly wimp tones.
He got a warm smile from the matronly woman with the bright
lips, an' a wave of recognition from her son, the broad-shoul-
dered deputy. He didn't pay Ed much mind, account of pokin'
around in the barrel of his rifle, gettin' ready for the hunt. Ed
looked for the same brand of anti-freeze he bought every winter,
ever a man of habit. He checked his spare change, thought better
of it, then strolled to the counter to make an order for next morn.
"Goin' out on the hunt with Frank tomorrow, Bernice?", he
enquired, knowin' the lady to be a pretty sharp shot herself.
"No fun for us ladies, Ed", she bewailed, her face a mask of
mock misery. "Someone's gotta mind the store while the boys go
out and let off steam."
"That case", he let his slope eye descend into a wink, "you won't
say no to coming out ice-skating with me this evening."
"Ohh Ed", she laughed at his tease, "as if I could ice skate!"
"Well, neither can I", he nodded. "Come along with me an' we'll

hold one another up."

Bernice laughed an' her son shook his head. "You're a cornball, Ed, always the same old lines. Tell you what... while you're out iceskatin', I'm gonna bring myself home Wisconsin's all-time record giant deer, and I'll buy you a beer with the prize money. But Mom...", he wrapped his arm around Bernice's shoulders, "... you've gotta stay here an' mind the store. No iceskatin'."

Ed made sure his anti-freeze would be ready next mornin', then wished 'em both a good weekend. After leavin' the store, Ed felt in the mood to give himself a treat. He went to the drug store an' gulped down two chocolate sodas, one after the other. Bought a couple of detective mags, then decided it was time for a beer.

In the Plainfield tavern, while lingerin' over his lite brew, the bartender asked him whether he'd be out huntin' next day.

"Maybe", he reflected. "But I don't reckon for deer. Never did have the heart to shoot those creatures down, truthfully."

"That a fact, Ed?", the bartender came back. "Howsabout those packages of venison you're always givin' away, instead of hard cash? I bet they just get up an' butcher 'emselves, right?"

"Oh", he wiped the foam for his mouth, an' got up ready to go, "I don't often kill much of that myself."

The huntin' season opened with a fine layer of frost on the ground. Ahead of Wisconsin's seasonal snowfall, the woodlands had the look of a magical fairyworld about 'em. Elmo Ueeck, out deerstalkin' alone, saw his chance when a fat, big-antlered buck trotted its way along the edge of the remain' Gein acres. Hit 'im square on, knocked him down an' finished him with one more shot. There was no way this docile old beast was gonna bag prizes. Wonder he'd lived so long in the first place. Still, Elmo was feelin' a little conscious of havin' caught game on Ed's property. He knew the little guy didn't take kind to anyone takin' that kind of liberty. But right then, who should come hurtlin' down the road, goin' at least 50 miles per hour, but little Ed himself. Elmo felt bad, caught right in the act an' all, but Ed just gave his thin-mouthed smile an' went rattlin' on by. Damnedest thing -

thought Elmo, laughin' - Ed normally drives so slow you can virtually walk faster.

Later that day, Ed invited himself over to the Hills' place. He knew that Lester would be out bangin' bucks with the rest of the boys, but it was a rare thing when he could resist the kind of fare Irene set out on a Saturday suppertime. She had her daughter an' son-in-law over, layin' on a hearty meal of pork chops an' macaroni with pickles, followed by cookies an' washed down with plenty of coffee.

Back at the weigh-in, while empty-handed Lester was lookin' forward to a supper of grocery store meat, Frank Worden came runnin' up an' tugged at Artie Schley by the arm.

"Hell is it, Frank?... You taken some buckshot in your pants?"

"It's Mom", Frank blurted out before the rest of the boys had stopped sniggerin', "I can't find her!"

Schley took Frank's panic to be the over-concern of a loyal son, protective of his genial ol' widowed mother. But, all the same, if he insisted she wasn't at home, and Muschinsky himself reckoned that the hardware store had been closed since the mid-morn, then they better give it a curs'ry check. She was probably over with one of the other guys' wives now, chatterin' away an' not realisin' it'd be before hungry Frank was on his way home, no game in tow. When they broke open the store door, it was just as empty as he'd expected it to be. Little too empty, in fact.

The store counter was turned to an angle, like someone had been movin' things around. "You see anything missing, Frank?" Schley was suddenly aware that Frank was nervy as hell, and that maybe he oughta be takin' this seriously. "Cash register", Frank nodded with agitation, "someone's come an' taken the cash register." Schley moved around the perimeters of the store, tryin' to think like a professional lawman. All that caught his eye was the well-stocked rifle rack, with a .22 calibre huntin' rifle slightly askew.

"There's blood down here, Arthur", Frank whispered below his breath like he could barely be forced to say it. "I said there's

blood, Art, what are we gonna do about it, for Christ's sake?!"
He was down on his hands an' knees, sniffin' at the red droplets
as if he could identify whether it was Mom's by his sense of
smell.

Schley felt that he suddenly had a spotlight on him - that Frank
was holdin' him responsible for ev'rything. From drivin' timber
trucks to a possible murder investigation in one 12-month. An'
all he could think to do was reach to that cockeyed deerstalker
rifle, to smell the barrel. As he did, an empty cartridge clattered
out on the floor. His deputy made an icy intake of breath.

"I think this may the rifle that, uh, possibly injured your mother,
Frank... I need you to tell me if anyone came in the store this
morning, that you know of..."

"How in hell would I know, I was out huntin' with you!", he
bawled with rage, on the edge of tears. Just then, his eyes fixed
on the counter.   "This cash receipt... it's a fresh one. "Anti-
freeze @ 99c", made out with this morning's date to Ed Gein...
Why, that bare-faced little rat!"

Schley tried to keep Frank's temper down on the ground.
"Steady, Frank... we don't know that Ed has anything to do with
this. We'll take a run over the ol' place now, have ourselves a
word. See if he can offer us a lead."

"... Askin' Mom whether she was goin' hunting with me today,
plain as day. Little runt probably planned to raid the store all the
time, just 'cos he don't make no money from that broken-down
farm of his anymore!"

"Second thoughts, I want you to stay here at the store... If you
get any word on your mom, I'll be back from the woods within
the hour." Frank protested, but Schley insisted he would
interveiw Ed without him or not at all. This was not gonna be a
usual openin' to the huntin' season.

"Hey, have you heard?", called out Jim Vroden, Irene's son-in-
law, in a burst of still-youthful excitement. Deputy Worden's
mother has gone missing. It's all over town. Someone broke into

her hardware store an' held her up. All that's left behind is a pool of blood an' some bulletshells - they say someone's killed her for sure!"

Irene screwed up her face in distaste, collectin' the plates as Ed wiped his clean with bread. "What in the world are we coming to? And you shouldn't go announcing someone's death before anyone's seen the evidence with their own eyes, Jimmy!... Poor Bernice", she dwelled on a recent memory of the middle-aged woman she'd attended school an' grown up with. "I can't believe anyone in Plainfield would do anything to hurt her."

"Sounds like a cold-blooded one all right", commented Ed, wipin' his lips. There was little doubt in his mind what had become of her, an' he said as much. "Bernice Worden eh?... Just to think, I was in her store only last night. Damnedest thing when it happens to someone you know".

"Why Ed", Irene looked at him with curiosity an' somethin' like pity. "How come every time someone gets banged on the head an' hauled away, you're always around? Weren't you in Pine Grove the night before that Hogan woman disappeared?... I declare, Ed, you're a regular bad luck charm."

A mile or so down the road, at the Gein farmhouse, Sheriff Schley and Deputy Sharkey were about to learn just how much bad luck a modest guy like Ed can bring you.

"You hear me, Eddie, I said it's Artie Schley here... just need to talk for a couple of minutes. Will you open on up?" Schley timed Ed for another minute on his wristwatch, though he was pretty sure the little guy wasn't home.

"What you say, Sheriff, we break in the back door?"

Schley frowned, not havin' enough experience in these matters to know whether bustin' in without a search warrant was justified. "Nah... Say, haven't I seen some kind of old outhouse built on the back of the building? Let's go see if there's an entrance through there."

If there was, they couldn't see it in the murky half-light. Like ev'ry other part of the Gein place, it was swathed in darkness.

"Goddam this thing..." Schley went first, blind leadin' the blind. "Ol' Ed's got a deer or a buck hung up here. Hold that door open, we ain't ever gonna find our way 'til..."
The bitter, icy sunlight shone in, an' Art Schley felt his senses needed adjustin'. The deer that hung feet-up from the rafters had a too-human look. It hung with a neat, red split all the way down from belly to chestplate to bowels. Cleaned out, gutted proper, just the way a deer should be. But not even the fleshiest doe had plump ol' titties hangin' down like that. An' a pale, wrinkled, butt. Schley leant back 'gainst the wooden beam, tryin' to come to terms. "I think we've found Mrs. Worden", he managed to gasp out in one deep breath. His deputy had already made up his mind on that one, pukin' like his life depended on it. The female body hung stark naked, steel meathooks through the sinews of the ankles. Schley had to assume it was Bernice Worden, bein' as the head was nowhere to be seen. Hacked clean away, leavin' the gore spillin' from her shoulders. He couldn't help but ponder how she might have won first prize at Muschinsky's weigh-in...

Schley got a friendly welcome when he called over at the Hills' place. Irene offered him coffee, an' some of the food left over from supper. He could only shake his head, politely decline while his stomach turned a somersault. "Have you found where Bernice has got to, Artie?", she asked if it was just some conversational pleasantry. "'Fraid we have", he nodded grimly. "I've just sent Burt Sharkey over to talk with Frank."
Irene kept her mouth open wide an' licked her fingertips, unwillin' to ask whether it had all come to the worse.
"Have you seen Eddie Gein at all, Mrs. Hill?... I'm gonna need to speak with him."
"Why, surely I have", Irene effused, graspin' at straws of normality. "He's right through in our living room, digesting his supper. Do you need a word with him now, Arthur?"
"Sure do", Schley growled as she led him through from the kitchen.

The ill-fated Mrs. Worden, shortly before her murder...

...and on the evening following her death.

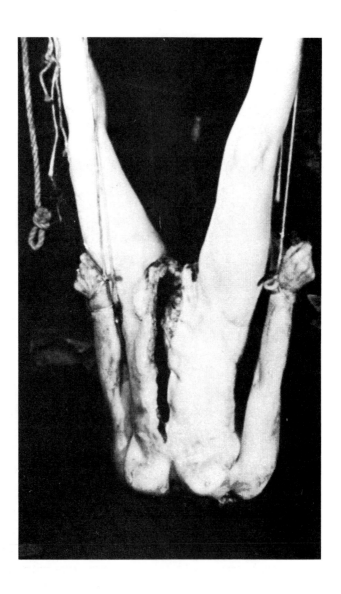

In the livin' room, the family watched **I Love Lucy** through a snowy screen. Ed was sat back in his chair, strokin' his little belly content as a fat kitten. "Howya doin' Art?", he called, with no sign of alarm.

Schley grimaced an' skipped the niceties. "Okay, Ed", he motioned a long arm forward, "get your hat and coat. You're coming with me."

"Where to?" The little guy looked just as bewildered as the family whose attention they'd grabbed.

"Wautoma - we're going to the county jail."

Ed looked blank, Schley wanted to choke him for feignin' incomprehension. "But I don't wanna go to Wautoma."

"If you stay here, you're gonna be lynched." The sheriff fought hard to control his temper, as the awful truth dawned on the faces of the onlookers. "Look, Ed... I'm taking you away for your own good. I've just come from your summer kitchen."

"Oh." No confession, no emotin'. He just got up slowly an' adjusted his hat, ready for leavin'.

Before settin' out for Wautoma, Schley locked Ed in the car an' called up his few part-time deputes, Frank Worden excepted. He told 'em to force entry to the Gein house, request the assistance of the State Crime Laboratory an' the county fingerprint man. Hell was about to spill its guts.

Word got round a shell-shocked town that Ed had been runnin' some kinda "murder factory" back at the old place. Police were comin' in from all over the county - Wautoma, Pine Grove, La Crosse - an' found too much horror for 'em all to handle. By the end of that black Saturday, the local uniform boys were sayin' they reckoned on seven victims bein' dispersed about the place. This was before Ed came clean on his ecological recyclin' activities, 'a course. And, truth be known, they really didn't have much idea of quantity. If someone was straightforward enough to ask how they were piecin' the bodies together, they'd just kinda shrug. There was an abundance 'a parts an' a distinct lack 'a wholes. Early Sunday morn, a guy from the state crime lab, name 'a Wilimovsky, came to take a squint at the corpus delicti. With a purely professional sense of morbid fascination, he photographed poor Bernice Worden's remains. It was still hangin' there in the outhouse, no-one darin' to remove it.

"Do we have any indication of what happened to the rest of this woman?", he called to uniformed men still scoopin' up bits of skin an' bone. He just got a fingerpoint for an answer, none 'a the nauseated cops able to match his keenness by now.

"And what is that, exactly?"

On top of a pile of Ed's five an' dime store possessions lay a crumpled suit. Baggy, wide-lapelled, a decade old an' not well-preserved. "I think they mean you should take a look inside it", advised D.A. Kileen, himself just about acclimatized to the all-pervadin' craziness. Folded inside the suit was a bundle 'a newspaper, headed by the obituary page from the local Plainfield rag. Like a package of fresh eel the fishmonger might sell ya - only this held more warm offal than a Scotch haggis.

"Is this her?", Wilimovsky winced, resistin' the urge to cover his nose.

"We believe it's some of her", came back Kileen. It was a genuine shitful a' raw intestine, with a few moist organs thrown in to boot. The forensics man folded it back up carefully, makin' a note of Exhibit A that would keep hauntin' his dreams. Careful not to appear phased, he scoured the grime-caked floor for more items among the chaos an' debris.

The cops were shiftin' ev'ry damn thing, like the systematic clearin' of a dead miser's sqalor. Wilimovsky checked off a few items - ball of rubbery material, possibly bubblegum; Dr. Pepper can half-filled with congealed liquid, possibly blood. They carried out a pair of tattered mattresses, an' an old burlap sack fell out from between 'em. It was steamin'.

"Hold it. Don't move it." No-one was disobeyin' orders. Wilimovsky reached in an' dragged out a two-foot lenth of twine. Hangin' from it was a human trophy Her hair was dark, dirty,

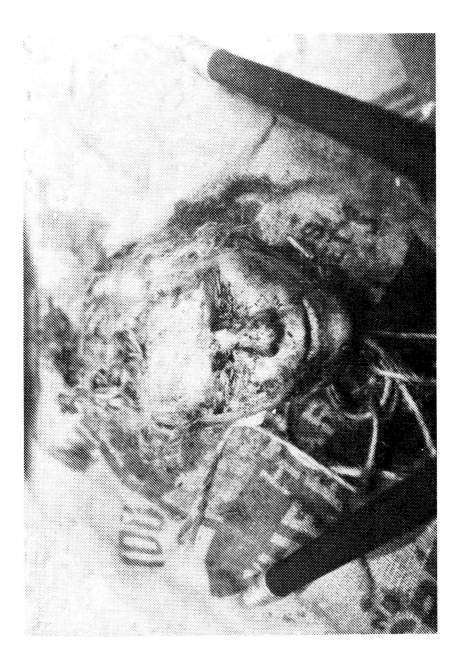

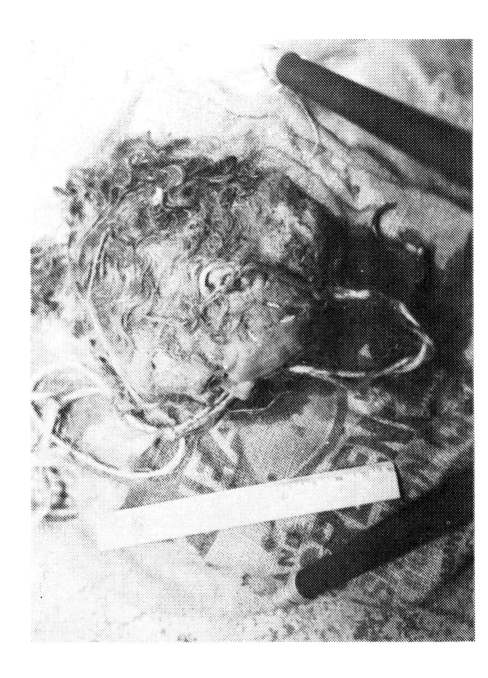

matted with blood. Her eyes were peacef'ly closed, but she had a dry plasma moustache formed by her two clogged nostrils. The twine was connected, as if holdin' a picture frame, by two long, rusty nails, driven deep into her eardrums.

"This her?", shouted Wilimovsky.

"Yeah... That's her", said Deputy Sharkey.

As the chief investigators left the farmhouse, the whole media circus was wheelin' its way into town. Not just out-of-state newspapermen, but TV an' radio reporters from all coasts. Kileen was the first big cheese of law enforcement they got their own hooks into. Unmindful of Frank Wordern, currently under sedation an' bein' tended by relatives, he gave a detailed description of how Ed had broken Bernice down to the sum of her parts. "What do you believe is Gein's motivation?", overrode an East Coast accent from behind a flash of camera bulbs. Kileen was about to decline an answer, when he got a flash of perverse inspiration. "We're not sure... but the crimes almost certainly seem to involve cannibalism." It was as sane a rationalization of craziness as he could manage. So the myth of Ed the cannibal was about to be born. America had its imagination grabbed by the gruesome details, but any rationale was just beyond comprehension. When Kileen met Ed at the county jail in Wautoma, the first questions to be asked were the most obvious.

KILEEN: "Did you kill Mrs. Worden, Ed?"

GEIN: "Maybe... I've been in a kind of daze. I know I went into the store that morning. Went in to get my anti-freeze. Paid her one dollar. She gave me a penny change. After that, I kinda suffered a mental blackout."

KILEEN: "Did you shoot her?"

GEIN: "I recall dragging the body across the floor of the store. I don't know if I shot her or hit her. I doubt that I shot her. I didn't have my gun with me."

KILEEN: "Do you recall removing and loading a rifle from the gun rack?"

GEIN: "No. Can't say as I can."

KILEEN: "Why did you steal the cash register. Did you need the money?"

GEIN: "No. I never even took the cash out of the register. I just wanted that register. I liked the way that little white roll of paper inside adds up all the items."

Kileen watched the little guy twitch under the burden of his own deranged logic. Told himself to bide his time - another coffee, another cigarette. Pretty soon, Gein's nerve wouldn't hold, an' the background of this whole sick, sorry affair would spill out.

"When you got Mrs. Worden's body home, you cleaned it and dressed it, just as if it had been a freshly-killed animal. Can you tell me why you did that?"

"I guess...", Ed gazed into his lap, seemin' to suppress a smile. "I guess I thought she was a deer."

Kileen crushed his paper cup. Sincere or not, tryin' to dig out Gein's motive was like tryin' to prospect for gold with a tooth-pick.

Years on, the stalemate would be the same. The rational mind pitted its logic 'gainst the now chubby little idiot-savant in the dock, an' lost. By this time, most were ready to believe Ed when he said how hazy his memory was. It had been eleven years, after all. Tempers had cooled, details had faded.

Yeh, folks were more willin' to accept, but they were no more capable of understandin'...

"Other than the details relating to events after Mrs. Worden was shot in the hardware store, were there any other times in your life that you had amnesia, or that you have no recollection of the events that happened?"

That was Mr. Sutton, the State Prosecutor. He was a nice feller - calm, courteous manner - though a little on the persistent side. Ed's counsel pointed out that if he had amnesia, he really wouldn't know about it, but the judge said No, he must answer. That was okay by Ed. He was never anythin' other than obligin'. "When I was sent to Central State, I wheeled in a patient for examination in the operating room.

He had a rectal examination, and they put in an expander
which caused bleeding. I almost passed out then."
Spectators smiled, raised their eyebrows, not sure whether to
give a wise nod or a sneer. Little Ed, hidin' away inside his
old-fashioned jacket, seemed just an innocent after all. The
Stan Laurel of the slaughterhouse.
Mr. Sutton didn't go for any of it. "Are you trying to tell me,
Eddie, that you don't remember anything you did to Mrs.
Worden before these photos were taken?"
The prosecutor held some pictures high for the court to see, a
voice called out "Exhibit A, your honor." Ed reserved judge-
ment 'til they were tight in his nervous little hands. Then he
made no bones. "Nope." He shuffled the black an' white
shots slowly, like a drunken man playin' a poker hand. "Uh-
uh." He shook his head.
Memory remained, but memory was a dream. How d'you
explain a time that was lived in twilight, to people who only
knew the day, an' took shelter from the night?
Sure, I hung her her up alright, but not like an animal. Like a
crucifixion in reverse. I'd hammered a wooden crossbar into the
hard bone just above the ankle. She hung ankle-up like a holy
offering, like a sacrifice. Took my hunting knife an' pushed it all
the way through the meat, into the plate of her sinful, cow-like
chest. Then I twisted an' took it down... Down, 'til she was ready
to unload. 'Til she was ready to spill all the sinful baggage God
has cursed a woman with - all the fleshly blessings she's been
granted, but is too sinful to be trusted with. Carved her with
loving, from the breast down to the pubic bone... AND I SAW A
WOMAN SIT UPON A SCARLET COLORED BEAST, FULL OF
NAMES AN' BLASPHEMY! HAVING SEVEN HEADS AN' TEN
HORNS... The gut muscles gave way like so much fat. I eviscer-
ated her, cleansed her of earthly sin. Her lady-breasts were tilted
upward. Guess that was 'cos they were defying gravity. They
pointed their motherly nipples at me, but I resisted.
Even in the heat 'a that moment, I know I resisted...

THE WOMAN WAS ARRAYED IN PURPLE AN' SCARLET COLOR, HAVING A GOLDEN CUP IN HER HAND FULL OF ABOMINATIONS AN' FILTHINESS OF HER FORNICATION...
I left the breasts be. Didn't seem right, to take away the instruments that fed Jesus when he was a boychild. Which my Ma fed me with, and which all good an' holy women raise their sons with. Not that this woman, this Worden woman, was anything but a Jezebel. I never made her suffer, only made her die, an' that's the way God would've willed it...

She was a fat, bountiful temptress. I cleansed her pubic cavity like I was casting out demons. I was getting a sweat, feelin' a little icky, but I went on. Out! - come the spongy walls of her diaphragm, and the demon ain't got a refuge. Out! - squeezes the aorta, and her wicked bloodline is done forever. She hangs before me cleansed, purified at last... UPON HER FOREHEAD WAS A NAME WRITTEN, "MYSTERY, BABYLON THE GREAT, THE MOTHER OF HARLOTS AND ABOMINATIONS OF THE EARTH!"

Truly don't recall what use I had for the rest of her. Her heart, I left that to soak in a saucepan, and her liver...

A feller has to think these things through real careful. I broke for supper first, over at the Hills' place. Irene Hill surely used to rustle up some delicious porkchops.

In the courtroom, nearly five minutes passed before Sutton gently took the photos from the little guy's hand. When it came time for adjournment, he declaimed in the transcriber's ear: "Did you see how he gloated over the evidence? I swear I've seen guys take less time ogling a Playboy centrefold."

Back in Plainfield, the house kept yieldin' up more surprises than a Christmas stocking. By Monday morn, the winter gave the woodlands a seasonal white blanket, four inches thick. It didn't stop the lawmen makin' an inventory of ev'ry item in the Gein collection. The previous day, Kileen stated that four fully intact human heads had been found, an' that forensics teams would be

tryin' to match 'em with other parts of the body. But this jigsaw just kept on growin'. Wilimovsky insisted that ev'ry last piece of crud, ev'ry vile, stinkin' piece of refuse should be mulled over for evidence. It gave results. Garbage sacks, that reeked like wasted food or cat litter, were found to contain more mouldin' human domes. Inside the worn frame of his bed was found more used bubblegum, the pickin's of his nose, an' a rotten head sawed off at the jawbone. There was even one de-capped sister restin' her lips 'gainst the skirtin' board, just waitin' to be discovered when the furniture got carried out. Seemed he'd got bored with her an' tossed her to one side. Monday afternoon, reporters from Time, Life and Look magazines made for a full-scale press invasion. When they collared hold of Deputy Sharkey, he added his ten cents worth of conjecture. "We know we have at least eleven dead", he told 'em. "There might be fifty for all we know."
An' the goods just kept on comin'. On Friday, November 29, the day after Thanksgiving, Sheriff Wanerski of Portage County was still lookin' for the further remains of Mary Hogan. True, they had what appeared to be her face, an' a skull which checked out with a car accident x-ray she'd had years back, but the rest of that woman was darned elusive. He'd had a garbage trench dug up alongside the farm. Came up with a complete skeleton, no ribcage, but a distinctive gold tooth. It was a pretty big body, leadin' to speculation that it might've been a male drifter who disappeared from the county back in the early '50's. But no - Ed was nothin' if he wasn't consistent. This was another lady, liber-ated from the graveyard back in Ed's diggin' days. The last yield the house gave up was when timber workers found some dogs diggin' up bones. If they hadn't been stopped, they'd have had a field day - the bones came from a human ribcage, arms, legs, an' a pelvis. This was in May, 1960.
On the mornin' of Friday, November 22, 1957, Kileen took Ed before Judge Herbert A. Bunde in Wautoma. He was charged, technic'ly, with robbery, bein' remanded on $10,000 bail. Kileen held back the murder charge, as he wanted Ed's sanity determined

first. Judge Belter appointed a local attorney named Belter as the defence, who straightaway entered a plea of not guilty by reason of insanity. The judge directed Ed should be held under pschiatric observation at Central State for 30 days. It was the start of a longer tenancy than anyone could then anticipate.

In downhome Plainfield, feelin's continued to run high. The town mayor protested to Kileen over Ed's speedy committment. As Wisconsin had never had capital punishment, there was a strong feelin' that Ed should have his ass hauled into jail, 'stead of facin' the "soft option" of a mental asylum.

That wasn't the way the psychiatric pros saw it. They wanted him under the microscope. Dr. Alfred P. Solomon of Chicago, one of the examinin' shrinks, stated that "Gein's case offers a rare opportunity for science to get many answers to anti-social behaviour. There is a much deeper motivation for these crimes than appears on the surface. A thorough study of this man could contribute very much to the field of psychiatry."

Consensus was that Ed consciously loved his mother an' loathed all other women, account of them never reachin' her high moral standards. Unconsciously, he loved other women, an' hated Augusta to Hell. All the same, he wanted her back to life, an' his resurrection hobby gave the illusion he needed. But, his frustrations arise, so he cuts up the bodies...

As rational explanations go, it ain't too bad. But anyone who can read our boy's actions should realise his waters flow a lot deeper than rationality can reach. It's true he wanted to raise the dead - in ways much closer akin to a tribal shaman than to Burke an' Hare - but it's also true that the indignities he performed on those dead women were born partly by his own spirituality. Ed had his own religion that was nothin' to do with Ma's piety - it was the extollation of his fantasies, his wish fulfillment, an' a hidden folk memory of dark pagan wildness. It was the eruption of a terrible spiritual potency, the type few men - "sane" or "insane" - ever experience. In truth, it was the only potency he ever person'ly knew or felt.

Among the hand-crafted household the cops found were some soup bowls. Ed made an art outta consumin' Campbell's tinned soup before Andy Warhol even thought of it. He'd stripped some heads down to the bare skull, pared off the top of the cranium an' supped his broth straight from the brainbowl. During his psychiatric examinations, he testfied that he got the idea from "reading about an old Norwegian custom". He got asked a lot of questions about the items that had freaked the lawmen out the most - his "extensive collection of female genitalia", as Judge Gollmar was to call it. Seems Ed had tried to preserve his collection of naked raw vulvas in salt, but found some of 'em went sickly green anyway. "I never was much expert at curin' meat. That was Ma's speciality, I kind of let that side of things slide." He took a mouthful of the apple pie his interrogators fed him on while they spoke. "Touched one with silver paint, and that kept it from goin' bad. Made it a little hard and brittle though." As Kileen an' the examinin' psychiatrist eyed one another, Ed started to grimace. Bein' as extreme facial expressions were such a rarity, the DA thought this might be one of the spasms of remorse an' self-pty he'd been allowin' himself, 'til Ed explained.
"Cheddar cheese on this apple pie... it's so dry", he whined. "Makin' me feel icky just to eat it."

Among the police who converged on the Gein farm was Chief Detective Weber, of the La Crosse Police Department. He'd come, hopef'ly, to close the file on a disappearance that took place in his town one October Saturday, 1953. On this day, Ed was makin' a visit to his aunt in La Crosse, lonely for a maternal stand-in. Fifteen-year old girl named Evelyn Hartley went missin' two blocks away, babysittin' for a local college professor an' his wife. No clues, but a pool of blood found in the garage. Now, all the local cops thought his looked hopeful. A young girl's dress was found amongst Ed's belongin's, all the circumstances fitted snug as a bug. But Weber seemed won over by Ed's pathetic charms. After the two of 'em spoke, the lawman told the press he was inclined to believe ev'rything Ed told him. He spoke of Ed's graverobbin' sessions - "whenever he felt one coming on, he would pray, and sometimes the prayers snapped him out of it."

"How about the cannibalism, detective?"

"I don't believe that at all", Weber waved off the suggestion. "I put some pretty strong questions to him, and he replied in the negative."

"Eating the flesh and drinking the blood", Ed pondered. I never felt capable of doin' that. That's kind of a Catholic thing, isn't it? I don't think my mother would have approved."

Seemed that the tennis shoes found near the scene of Evelyn's disappearance were much too big for Ed, an' that was good enough for Weber. But what seemed to sway him mostly was that he realised Ed was a pitiful monster. "You'd never believe he would be the kind of guy to do such a thing. You feel like he needs help awful bad."

On December 23, Judge Bunde announced the observation period had led state psychiatrists to conclude Ed was insane. He was committed permanently to Central State, an' stayed there 'til, in January '68, the hospital superintendent advised Judge Gollmar he was mentally competent to stand trial. The past was about to be dug up all over again, not for the the first time, By November 14 of that year, Ed was found guilty of first-degree murder. This was for the killin' of Bernice Worden, though the fact that he offed Mary Hogan was technic'ly admitted. Then, under Wisconsin's peculiar laws, the sanity hearin's had to start all over again. Just like ev'ryone expected, Ed was judged crazy as a loon again, an' packed off to Central State for an indefinite period.

While he was settlin' in at the hospital, one of the male nurses had to come an' tell Ed what the state of Wisconsin proposed to do with his possessions. Attorney Belter had been appointed guardian of his estate, an' ordered to auction off all Ed owned to placate the families of the dead an' the desecrated. It didn't amount to a whole lot. His furniture, pots & pans, rusted farm equipment. An' any musical instruments that were still in workin' order - zither, harmonica, accordian. Ed would never serenade the dead again. There were also his motor vehicles - his 1949 maroon Ford sedan, his 1940 pick-up truck, an' a white Ford sedan. No-one ever remembered him drivin' the white Ford, though one was seen in the vicinity the night a young girl disappeared from Jefferson, Wisconsin...

As a means of compensatin' the good townsfolk, it kinda backfired. The date set was March 30, 1958 - Palm Sunday. The local clergy were outraged. "Great nations have grown up and disappeared, and in practically every case it was because the people ignored the laws of God", a preacher warned like he could see the Four Horsemen on the horizon. "For any nation that forgets God, that nation will God destroy." Damnation was on its way.

Just a few months on, Ed was startin' to recall his isolated life at the farmhouse with mixed feelin's. At the hospital, ev'rything was made sharply visible by bright, sterile, electric light. He'd spent so many years in true darkness, colorin' his own strange misdeeds with the shades of his imagination. He imagined what it would feel like for the lawmen who went searchin' the place. To shine their torches an' illuminate scenes that only belonged in a world of darkness. On the living room wall, they shone a light on a cheap ol' picture of Jesus, gazin' up at Angel Gabriel. A pile of old children's books on the floor stood next to a copy of **Gray's Anatomy**. Then there were the skulls in the summer kitchen...

The cardboard box in the main kitchen, where a disgusted patrolman had found a collection of gristly, peelin' noses.

The furniture removal guy had felt faint when he'd reached to grip on Ed's dinin' room chairs, an' touched his hand into greasy, lumpy fat. Upholstered with human flesh, ev'ry one of 'em. He couldn't even bring himself to sit down an' get a grip.

The lampshades were fashioned from thin, dermatitic skin.

The waste basket was made from a human bread basket.
A huntin' knife sheath was so organic it was almost like a dead guy's pecker.
A Quaker Oats box was fulla scraps of decayin' head integuement.
"... Oh, what in God's name is this?", hollered a visitin' captain from Wautoma, too sickened to take in what he was seein' anymore. 17 fleshy bobbles hung on a hand-fashioned leather belt. Like pink warts, erogynous hickies, or... "Damn me to hell if that lunatic hasn't made himself a belt of titties!"
Sheriff Schley, over from speakin' with Ed at Wautoma, stood alone in the torchlit kitchen. "This is just too horrible. Too darn horrible for words" was all he kept sayin', words he echoed for the press. He needed more light in that place. Its oppressiveness was makin' him feel just a little crazy himself. He tugged on the stiff cord of the kitchen blind, an' found it blowin' him a kiss. "Oh Jesus shit!... What?... What in hell?..."
The contraction of the blind had brought two severed female lips together. Painted red, voluptuous, like amorous strips 'a pepperoni.
The world ain't seen too many craftsmen like Ed.
As the frensics men counted out all nine of his vulva collection, they noted the deference he'd paid to his latest flame. All tied up an' squashed, she had a red ribbon wrapped around her from the remainin' pubic hair to the inner membrane. And he'd kept more of her, a chunk of raw anus attached like a symbol of fleshy favoritism.

"Eddie, there's something you really ought to know", the administrator of his psychiatric unit spoke softly to him. It was the 21st of March, nine days 'fore the scheduled auction. "Last night, it seems a group of people... they don't know who, ex-actly... set light to your home, the farmhouse that is. They burned it down."
Ed was cleanin' up, preparin' for the day ahead, when he got the .

news. He paused for a moment before gettin' with his chores.
"Just as well", he said.

Chapter Six
PSYCHO-CELEBRITY

**"There was an old man named Ed,
who wouldn't take a woman to bed.
When he wanted to diddle,
he cut out the middle,
and hung the rest in the shed."
A "geiner" - popular sick jokes with the young people
and children of Wisconsin in the late '50's and early '60's.**

Ed was the complete model patient. Never needed any of the
tranquilizers they used to zombify the poor lunatics, an' he was
about as helpful as helpful can be. Even used to wheel the more
unstable patients around from ward to ward. New nurses an'
orderlies used to get taken aside and told by their workmates as
soon as they arrived:
"That's Ed Gein!"
"Why... that little old guy? But he looks so harmless, like he
couldn't hurt anyone."
Nor could he. In a hospital environment, where he could be
regulated an' ordered around just like a kid, he had some of that
child-like sense a' security he remembered from before his imagination went berserk. His religion was still there, but it was way ,
way below his skin. Augusta too - he'd never regard anyone with
such fondness as when he remembered his dear, sacred Ma, but
she no longer felt like such an all-dominatin' power.
What ruled his life now was routine. Sad to say, but institutional
livin' agreed with the little wild man. While Wisconsin kids were
bein' told by their mothers, "If you don't behave, Ed Gein will get
you!", Ed was knucklin' down to the menial chores he'd always
performed. Given time, he put his dexterity to better use with
carpentry, sewin' an' weavin'. Quite the craftsman once more,
though he'd never find such exotic raw materials again. He put
on weight, enjoyin' ev'ry meal prepared for him, turnin'

nothin'down. He read just about ev'rything in the hospital library. Though the subjects of murder an' grave robbery were thin on the shelves, he could still bone up on his anatomy. Geographical books, an' travel fiction, became his most abidin' obsession.

In the outside world, he was becomin' a monster of popular myth. The kids told "geiners" - "Ed Gein is trav'ling on a bus. He walks up behind a woman an' gooses her butt. She says, "Hey, cut that out!". He says, "Why gee, thanks'" was about the least worst.

Inside Central State, he was a well-liked, amicable little guy. Absent-minded but obligin', shufflin' round goin' nowhere fast with his eyes glued to the floor.

But food an' shelter weren't always enough. When he took the stand again in '74, he was optimistic he'd make it back to the outside world on the grounds of a return to mental health. In the wonderful world of movies, sev'ral mythic madmen were now based on him, but he was shielded from, or unint'rested by the fact. When friendly ol' Judge Gollmar asked him why he felt so ready for release, he replied it was because "some of the doctors told me so." When asked what his plans were, he said he'd worked as a carpenter, mason an' hospital attendant, an' could do most anythin'. "Work", he said, "is an important issue today. In some places, more fellers want to work than there is work. And in other places, it's the other way round."

Ed had given his role in the modern world serious consideration, but not ev'ryone was impressed. The judge bore in mind the understatement by Ed's attorney in the '68 trial - "I don't think he has a full appreciation of what he has done."

The director of Central State's psychiatric board was cautious. "Under careful conditions, Mr. Gein would be all right. Under stress, I feel he would revert to his psychosis."

Four examinin' shrinks from Central State countered his claim to be ready for release. Two recommended a more lib'ral regime, sayin' he should be committed to Winnebago State Hospital, where "he would be helped to adjust to more complex circumstances." The two others opposed this all they could, objectin' to the accessibility of women.

Ed sat up straight an' dignified in his vintage jacket to hear the judge's rulin'. Gollmar shook his whiskery head, and, with a sense of sadness t'ward the little guy in question, pronounced: "I don't think Mr. Gein has the strength to cope with society. I don't think he ever had the strength to cope with society. He would be a pathetic, confused, out-of-place individual in society today. Because of the enormity of his crime, and the enormity of the others alleged to him, I doubt very much whether the majority of people want such a person in society."

The accompanyin' male nurse from Central State moved to pat Ed on the arm. He didn't seem much phased. The judge adjusted his readin' glasses an' turned to Ed:

"You know, Eddie, you would find the world terribly frustrating.
his readin' glasses an' turned to Ed:

"You know, Eddie, you would find the world terribly frustrating.
People might not be very good to you. It's sort of a Rip Van Winkle situation. Simply crossing the street in a big city, or getting food, would prove very difficult after many years in an institution. I fear you would be exploited if you were released, I could see you becoming "Exhibit A". The public has not forgotten this matter, Eddie. It continues to be a sensational thing. I know that, if you had stood trial in 1957 for the murder of Mrs. Worden, you would have been eligible for parole in 1967. But those were not the circumstances. I wish I knew of a way to give you more freedom, but I don't. I'm afraid I must reject the petition."

"Thank you sir." As the court rose, Ed called to the judge, without irony. "Thank you for your kind consideration."

In the car, on the way back to Central State, the nurse tried to commiserate. "How you feelin', Eddie?"

"Okay." He nodded, the faraway smile comin' back to his face. "I've got other matters to attend to. Got my round-the-world cruise to plan." His minder smiled, but Ed was serious. Ev'ry atlas, ev'ry travelogue, was stampin' itself on his subconscious. He was an interior trav'ler, makin' an internal map of a world he'd never known firsthand.

In 1978, Ed travelled lit'rally. Central State was turned into a "correctional facility", so he got transferred to the Mendota Mental Health Institute in Madison, Wisconsin. This was "by virtue of stable condition and a low security status." At the institute, the young nurses an' admin workers loved him. "Don't tell me... are you that Eddie Gein?" He didn't mind admittin' to it now. Maybe he didn't like diggin' up the past, but it was far enough away now to be just a dream. He became a novelty, a celebrity. They'd all tease the chubby, dreamy little guy - "Make sure Eddie gets a good lunch now. We don't want him sawing off anyone's arm while they're not looking" - but the biggest kick about it was how totally an' meekly harmless he'd become.

In 1979, an unshaven man in his thirties was dragged, howlin' obscenities, into a police station in Milwaukee, Wisconsin. "Sit 'im down", growled the interrogatin' officer, glarin' with disdain at the grinnin' wannabe-Manson.

"Recognise her?", he held out the first of a series of coroner's photos. An old woman, her face torn an' bludgeoned, had had her eye sockets gouged 'til they were nothin' but deep red holes. "Mabye I do", replied the smiler, in a theatrical sleazo voice. "But ya get to see so many dead ol' ladies, gets to be hard to tell 'em apart."

The officer looked at his sergeant. Could well be this was the crud they'd bin seekin'. Milwaukee had come a long way down the line since Happy Days.

"Her name's Helen Lows - 86-years old. Some piece 'a shit didn't like the possibility of her dyin' peacefully in grand old age. Beats her to death, then cuts patches out of her face. Any idea who we might be lookin' for?"

The psycho, Pervis Smith by name, couldn't resist proclaimin' his own celebrity. "You could be looking for me, I guess. That's if

you wanna find the guy who killed her, an' five hund'ed thousand
other ol' ladies!"
Could be just another confesser, but they were gonna take him at
face value. This guy smelled right.
"Say, what you do to her, Perv?... you don't mind if I call you
Perv, do you?... All these gashes, hairline scars, lacerations"...
He held up a series of pictures, all from contrastin' angles, all
equally ugly. Each showed a bloody crisscross pattern on a
dif'rent part of her face.
The smiler lost some 'a his shine. "I was gonna cut her face off...
Right off... Woulda done it too, if some buncha old crocks in the
next apartment hadn't come callin' at the door!"
They could feel this creep under their skin now. Things were
gettin' uglier, more convincin', all the time. "So... Where d'you
get that humdinger of an idea from?"
"Way back in Central State..." Smith's ego was on the rise again.
"Has a previous conviction for attempted murdere and assault
1974", broke in the sergeant. "Ruled mentally incompetent, sent
to Central State for four years."
"They obviously gave him some real effective treatment... What
the hell happened back there that made you wanna do this kinda
shit, Perv?"
"Oh, nothing happened." The psycho played to an invisible
camera for all he was worth. "Just got me some good tuition."
"... Tuition?"
"Sure", he started to cackle. Learned everything I know about
makin' a death mask out of a woman's face from my good friend,
Little Eddie Gein. Real friendly guy, oblige you any way he
can."

    In the cramped comfort of his room, darkness had come again
for Ed. It wasn't that the lights had died, just that since it'd got
harder to breathe, ev'rything had grown dim. They said the
illness may not pass, that he'd have to learn to live with it - he
was doin' his best. Never wanted to make any fuss.

He held his precious world atlas to this chest, an' thought of all the distance he'd covered. When he first came to Central State, he didn't truly know where he was. He was a little guy in a lot of trouble. Not knowin' where he stood, how he'd arrived there, or much about the world as other folks perceived it at all. He'd travelled a great distance since then.

He'd replayed the start of the journey in his head a thousand times - Ma, Henry, the loneliness, the women, - 'til he knew better than any doctor how he'd got from there to here. He'd retraced his internal route, knowin' the dark routes of passage far better than anyone possibly could.

There were so many strange stops along the way none of the doctors or the p'licemen had charted. He shut his eyes, an' remembered what Judge Gollmar had said:

"I'm very concerned that, out of the collection of female genitalia discovered at Mr. Gein's home, two of the preserved vulvas have proved to be of young women aged somewhere between twelve to eighteen. There were no girls of that age buried in the county during the period in question."

There'd been others - at least one other, though he couldn't truly remember how many now. Remembered her name was Georgia... She was a pretty little thing - fourteen, maybe fifteen - and he'd picked her up in Jefferson around the time he started visitin' graveyards. She was a feisty one all right, but once he'd made her quiet, she'd shown him the way to Heaven. To Godliness. He'd once read, in a book called **Psychopathia Sexualis**, about a guy named Ardisson - took a dead three-year old girl an' gave her "an embrace to wake the dead". Kinda thing the baser fellers called "eatin' pussycat", but this was on a cold body. Ed wanted to breathe life into the dead, but he wanted to do it the way God might. When he got Georgia's body home, he cut the sinful womanhood out of her pure white innocence, an' held it over his face. Through its fleshy vortex, he could see into the eyes of God.

The journey inside was over now. It had begun an' ended in

darkness.

EDWARD GEIN DIED FROM HEART AND RESPIRATORY
FAILURE ON JULY 26, 1984, WHILE SUFFERING FROM
CANCER. HE WAS 77. HE WAS LAID TO REST IN THE
ONLY AVAILABLE PLOT IN PLAINFIELD CEMETARY,
NEXT TO HIS MOTHER, AUGUSTA.

'Psycho'· model dies in asylum

MADISON, Wis. (AP) — Ed Gein, a farmer hospitalized nearly 27 years ago for the grisly slayings on which the movie "Psycho" reportedly was based, died today at a psychiatric institute.

Gein, 76, was found innocent by reason of mental disease in his only trial and spent almost all his life since 1957 in state mental institutions. He had been at the Mendota Mental Institute since May 1978, hospital officials said.

The events that led to Gein's arrest began on Nov. 16, 1957, after it was discovered Bernice Worden, 58, was missing.

A Wood County deputy drove to Gein's farm to ask if he had noticed anything. No one was home. He looked into a lean-to at the side of the house and saw Mrs. Worden's body hanging by the heels, decapitated and "dressed out like a deer," according to statements at the time.

Authorities arrested Gein in town. Searching his farmhouse, they found preserved human heads and lampshades and chair seats made out of human skin. But one room was boarded off: the room that had belonged to Gein's mother, who died in 1945. That room was just as she left it.

Police accused Gein of robbing the recently dug graves of women, who like his mother, died in middle age. They found a death mask of a woman who owned a rural tavern and had disappeared three years before.

Robert Bloch, the author of the novel· on which Alfred Hitchcock's 1960 thriller "Psycho" was based, lived about 50 miles from Gein's farmhouse and based his book on the episode, according to The Milwaukee Journal. Hitchcock's main character is obsessed by his dead mother and keeps her skeleton in his home.

Gein, after his arrest, was declared unfit to stand trial and was sent to Central State Hospital at Waupon.

In 1968, he was tried in the death of Mrs. Worden. It was ruled that he was insane at the time of the crime and he was returned to the hospital with a verdict of innocent by reason of mental disease or defect.

PART TWO
ED'S CHILDREN

*In the mid-1980's, the British tabloid press ran a story about a
female "approved school" (reformatory) teacher. who had
showed her charges the movie* **The Texas Chainsaw Massacre.**
*Described, predictably, by the press as a "video nasty" (a graphic
horror movie, such works being banned on video in Britain), the
film was not, at that time, banned. After a subsequent outcry in
the local press, which led to threats to remove her from her job,
she committed sucide by overdose. This section of the book is
dedicated to her, and to censors and superficial moralists everywhere.*

*It is also dedicated, with admiration, to the memory of
Anthony Perkins.*

Chapter One
NORMAN

"... And that is when I saw him,
as I pulled up to the side of a small hotel,
he was there..."
24 HOURS FROM TULSA - Bacharach & David
(as sung by Dusty Springfield)

In the late-50's, horror writer Robert Bloch was living in small-town Wisconsin. Having started his writing career in the classic 50's pulp, **Weird Tales**, as a protege of H.P. Lovecraft, he was now scratching a modest living as a professional novelist. At that time, supernatural horror was all but a thing of the past for him. He was finding his niche in a series of downbeat, psychological crime novels, that touched soley on the mortal side of the macabre. Titles were **"The Scarf"**, **"The Deadbeat"**, **"The Kidnapper"**, **"Firebug"**, **"Night-World"**, and **"The Block Ending"** - they all tapped the vein of bleak, small-town Americana, everyday scenarios where things could go hopelessly wrong. His dialogue was sharp and economical, the story normally containing a blackly humorous twist, like an americanised Roald Dahl or a grand guignol James M. Cain. He had his own style, but was yet to truly make his mark. Then...

"I was sitting in Weyaweuga, Wisconsin, a town so small that if you sneezed on the north side, somebody on the south side said "Gesundheit". Everybody knew everybody else's business. Some 40-odd miles away, in an even smaller town called Plainfield, someone walked into Ed Gein's shed on a Saturday morning and discovered a woman hung in the rafters dressed like a deer. The police arrested Gein, and suspected he may have murdered others, too. That's all our little weekly paper said, because it was not their habit to badmouth small-town living.

"I knew very little about the Gein case per se, and nothing whatsoever about him, except he was a 50-year old man, a respected citizen for his entire life. He had been a babysitter; he gave people little gifts (of "venison")). He had apparently been killing women for some time; there was talk on the local radio station about digging up graves. I was amazed that Gein could conduct himself without anyone suspecting the truth. I said, "there's a book here!"

"It started me thinking. I tried to figure out what kind of man could get away with murder, to develop a pattern for this imaginary character. I decided he was probably schizoid, It would be more plausible if he himself didn't know what was going on. What would motivate him? I came up with the Oedipal situation and the transvestite thing, which was pretty offbeat at the time..."

Offbeat, and almost telepathically perceptive, unless Mr. Bloch is exhibiting a selective memory. **"Psycho"** - the novel - is as sparse a narrative as you would expect from a pulp crime novel written in seven weeks. But it's great on the gritty detail, and petty paranoia, of small-town life. It also gave us Norman Bates, one of the great archetypes of popular fiction. We all know Norman - or think we do - that hyper-neurotic, super-sensitive mama's boy. An intense young man with an air of common decency about him, who would kill a young woman as soon as he looked at her...

But the Norman of the novel is an even more fucked-up (and far less attractive) character than the sympathetic anti-hero played by Anthony Perkins. He's uneducated but literate, and just about intelligent enough to recognise the source of his own problems. He tries to talk through his Oedipus complex with his mother, only to be rebuffed and mocked (though, as every asshole that's ever parked itself in front of a screen knows, Mother is all in the mind). He's also impotent, frustrated and misogynistic - *"That's the way girls were - they always laughed. Because they were bitches."*

Norman has bad eyesight, as a result of a bang round the head he received from Mother (left-brain damage, right-brain dominance

- do we have a pattern here?), whilst indulging in some narcissistic masturbation -

"It was nasty to stare at yourself, all naked and unprotected; to peek at the blubbery fat, the short hairless arms, the big belly, and underneath it..."

You may gather by this point that Slim Jim neurotic Tony Perkins wasn't chosen for his physical resemblance to the character. Hitchcock needed him to be a cute monster, the kind of psycho next door we could all love. As Bloch says, "You couldn't put Rod Steiger in that role and do it successfully on screen."

Unlike Ed, the real Psycho, Norman also has a history of institutionalization. Suffice to reiterate, he ended up alone in the motel when he poisoned Mother and her lover with strychnine, and was never the same after. Unlike Perkins' Norman, the original character's rage is mainly unleashed by drinking whiskey (fresh-faced Perkins looked like he never drank anything stronger than milk, though in his real life he was partial to the odd experiment with hallucinogens).

What both Normans have got in common, with each other and with Ed, is that they're avid readers. The novel's Norman verges on being a "literary man", though he likes his share of filth. He reads De Sade's **"Justine"**, **"La-Bas"** (Huysmans' story of an obsession with mass murderer and rapist, Gilles De Rais), and is *"mature enough to understand that he might be the victim of a mild form of schizophrenia"*. Perkins-Psycho's cultural inclinations are merely indicated by some classical LPs, and the Renaissance rape scene he dislodges in order to spy on Janet Leigh through a hole in the wall. But look what Norman is reading at the start of the novel -

"Grotesque but effective - it certainly must have been! Imagine flaying a man - alive, probably - and then stretching his belly to use it as a drum! How did they actually go about doing that, curing and preserving the flesh of the corpse to prevent decay?"

Familiar, eh? All the more remarkable then, that Bloch swears "it was inspired by the murders, not by Ed Gein, murderer. Years later, Anthony Boucher wanted me to do a factual crime piece on the Gein case for the Mystery Writers of America. In my research, I discoverd that Gein was schizoid, that he had a mother fixation, that he had lost his mother - I don't know if he dug her up again and stuck her in the cellar - and that he was a transvestite. However, he didn't wear his mother's clothes. He went Norman one better; Gein wore strips of skin and breasts cut from his victims. He also indulged in necrophilia, cannibalism, and a few other "isms" that weren't in the province of my character - and wouldn't have been very popular with readers in the '50's."

(The latter vices Bloch refers to are, of course, mythologised versions of Ed's shining career. The Norman character wove a couple of myths into the tapestry himself. When Hitchcock was interviewed by Francois Truffaut about **Psycho**, he was able to say that "it was based on the true story of a man who kept his mother's body in his house, somewhere in Wisconsin", this being a pop myth he helped create himself. Norman Bates also popularised the misconception that a schizophrenic is simply someone with a split personality.)

"The facts were amazing", says Bloch. "They even horrified me a little. I'm not going to look in mirrors for awhile. How can I come up with something that so closely parralels reality? What kind of a sickie am I?"

If his claims are accurate, he's the kind of sickie most cash-starved pop fiction writers would choke their grandma to trade places with. All the same, he was convinced that "this one would never be made into a movie!"

Then along came one revered British ex-pat Hollywood director, and a sensation-hungry public. **Psycho** was adapted for the screen by scriptwriter Joseph Stefano, otherwise notable for his work on the seminal SF series, **The Outer Limits**. He kept Bloch's basic plot structure - not revealing that Norman's malevolent mother is dead, and that he is really the killer, until the end of the story. Okay, it's old hat. But in its day, the Oedipal angle was mind-blowing. Only familiarity and pale imitation have bred contempt (one example of many is the 1966 monster movie, **It**, ostensibly about legendary Jewish folk demon the Golem, where mad curator Roddy Macdowall talks to the rotted corpse of his mother, kept in her bed...).

Stefano, who has a background in radio drama, merely added some sharp dialogue to Bloch's blueprint, and placed the emphasis on Marion Crane in the first quarter of the story, as played by the beautiful Janet Leigh.

Psycho was far closer in style to the Master's TV show, **Alfred Hitchcock Presents**, than to his glossy colour thrillers of the late 50's. Made in black & white, on a relatively low budget (around the $100,000 mark), it was notable for being one of the first movies to show the leading lady in her bra, and one of the very first to have her killed off in the first few reels. Hitchcock had latecomers barred from the cinema, in case they should wonder just where Ms. Leigh is. And when she dies, she dies horribly. A lot of blood has flowed under the bridge since then, but Psycho was one of the first movies to metaphorically jab pins in the audience's eyes. In the novel, Bloch has the hapless Marion (or Mary, as he called her) decapitated in the shower. Dramatic, but it's all over in the space of *"She saw the knife that would cut off her scream. And her head"*. As Bloch puts it:

"Writers, for the most part, didn't do gross things in those days. You could zing the reader with one line, then get out, instead of going into the murder sequence." But "neither were there de-capitations in those days" (in the cinema). "I wouldn't have wanted it that way anyway. Too messy."

Bloch's "don't give 'em any head" line would be belied by William Castle's **Homicidal**, one of the first post-Psycho thrillers (still tamely done, in comparison). Meanwhile, Hitchcock, and cinematographer Saul Bass, had to find a way to violate the viewer and appease the censor. Their compromise - a shower scene with the character naked but no explicit nudity, a bloodily

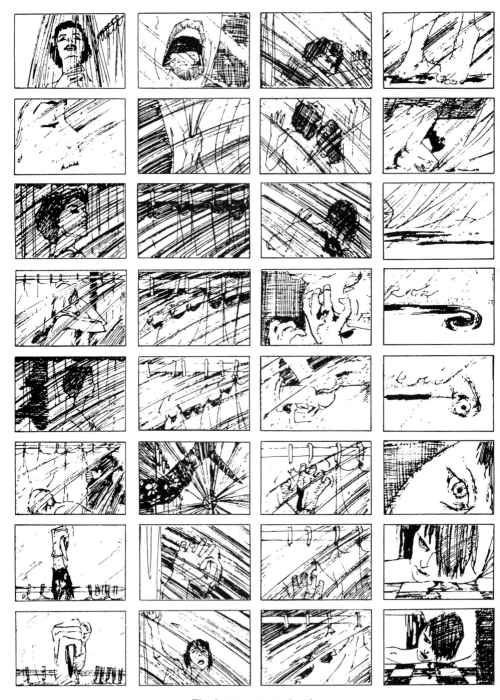

The shower scene storyboard -
blueprint for Janet Leigh's brutal
but celebrated demise, in **Psycho**

violent knife attack where the knife is seen to touch skin only once - hit the target, largely due to Bass's frenetic camera angles. Reviewers screamed moral disgust, but the appeal of the scene is far more masochistic than sadistic. That knife is coming at you. Whatever your sex, that's you in the shower, and, in your naked vulnerability, you just can't dodge the attack. Gallons of chocolate sauce in the bath made for convincing monochrome blood, and Janet Leigh died with gusto. Such convincing plasmatic carnage wouldn't hit the mainstream screen in colour 'til **Bonnie & Clyde**, in 1967, and **The Wild Bunch**, in 1969. At the other end of the critical scale, it made things possible for drive-in sickos like Herschell Gordon Lewis, with his **Blood Feast**. But what's most remarkable about **Psycho** is that it made a classic 50's/60's anti-hero out of, well, a psycho...

Psychological horror movies, while not yet then in vogue, had been creeping in over the last few years. Clouzot's **Les Diaboliques**, in 1955, had great fun with murder, a Dostoyevskian framework of guilt, a lesbian subtext, and a couple of well-loaded shocks. Michael Powell's **Peeping Tom**, released about six months before **Psycho**, shared with it, and with Fritz Lang's classic **M**, the burden of making a serial killer sympathetic. And, as with **Psycho**, it featured a personable and pitiful young man, who had an unfortunate compulsion to kill young women.

Perkins' Norman is an icon of our times. Cute, twitchy, easy to sympathise with, too neurotic to get close to. He has his mother's overtones of moral puritanism, which he tries hard to fight, the tension of this conflict leading him to kill. "They also pay who meet in hotel rooms", says Marion during the film's opening sexual liaison, not realising she is to be one of the first in a long cinematic line of naughty girls butchered by fucked-up men. Perkins plays Norman as a charmingly nervous, outgrown adolescent, partially removed from the sad, middle-aged grotesque of the novel. Despite a few incongruities (Norman must be one hell of a ventriloquist, considering the screaming matches he has with

"Mother", i.e. himself), repeated viewings show young Mr. Bates to be a black humorist of the first order. "She isn't quite herself today", he says of his moribund mother upstairs. When Marion refers to his taxidermy hobby, he confesses that "I hate the look of beasts when they're stuffed", enough though Mother has enough preservative chemicals in her to start a warehouse fire. At the movie's immortal ending, where Norman's facade of sanity has been totally blown in a padded cell scene, he registers on our hearts as one of the most loveable sickos in pop culture. His transvestism is dismissed in the closing scenes, as simply a self-deception that helps keep Mother alive. In the novel, there's no doubt he gets some visceral thrill from seeing his own chubby form in a dress. On screen, Norman's deranged grin leaves no doubt he is at least as far gone as both his fictional and factual inspirations. To dispel any doubt of where the character came from take a look at the end of Bloch's novel:

"Some of the write-ups compared it to the Gein affair up north, a few years ago... Written and oral rumours were circulating in which Norman Bates was protrayed as guily of cannibalism, Satanism, incest, and necrophilia."

Psycho became a yardstick for the psychotronic sixties, and Bloch signed away all screen rights for $6000. Perkins became typecast as a dangerous, twitchy neurotic - despite fine work in **On The Beach**, Orson Welles' version of Kafka's **The Trial**, and **Catch 22** - turning up as psychotic as ever in **Pretty Poison, Crimes of Passion** and **Edge of Sanity**.

And, of course, in all the **Psycho** sequels...

Mental illness came out to play at the cinema. Psychosis was fair game for exploitation, in movies ranging from classics like Polanski's **Repulsion**, Aldrich's **Whatever Happened to Baby Jane?** and **Hush, Hush, Sweet Charlotte** (old dames of Hollywood go ga-ga) to low budgeters like **Dementia 13** and **Strait-jacket** (written by Bloch himself). Whatever their respective merits, **Psycho** was still looked upon as their progenitor. In the days before a **Psycho II** would have been taken for granted, the very idea was sacrelige to film buffs. Splatter movie specialist Frank Henenlotter (**Basket Case, Brain Damage**) preceded his current career with a short entitled **Son of Psycho**. It consisted mainly of a hardcore gore re-shoot of the shower scene, with Dyan (**Ilsa - She-Wolf of the S.S.**) Thorne replacing Janet Leigh. In horror circles, it counted for something of a punk statement. Talking Heads, in the days when they sounded like a white funk Velvet Underground, released a great, twitchy little number called **Psycho Killer** - all the rock writers making comparisons between, thin, nervous, dark-haired singer David Byrne, and thin, nervous, dark-haired Tony Perkins. It was that much ingrained in the popular consciousness.

Then the unthinkable happened. A couple of young American enthusiasts named Gary Travis and Michael January announced plans, in the early '80's, for a film entitled **The Return of Norman**. Bloch was miffed, commenting that "Apparently these gentlemen have no realisation that there are such things as copyright laws and screen rights." Maybe not. But his own awareness of them didn't benefit him a great deal either.

As he had forfeited all rights to the title, he had to submit a sceenplay for **Psycho II** to Universal Pictures, who had bought out the rights to the first movie from Paramount.; They had also legally blocked the "Return of..." project. The screenplay was based on the same premise as his novel in progress of the same name:

"The sequel has a great deal more comment on our times than Psycho did. I began thinking about the violence in society. What would old Norman think if he were suddenly released into today's world?"

What indeed? Would a former serial killer be shocked by America's escalating crime rate? Whatever, Bloch is a socially conscious writer who does his best to criticise contemporary society, but is limited by the restrictions of his medium. Reading his **Psycho II** novel tells you he didn't like modern-day society in the '80's. Neither did he seem to care for it much in the '50's - one of his old, "noirish" novels included a long diatribe against the beat generation. As far as he could see, they were the epitome of everything negative, amoral, nihilistic. Their short-lived cultural rebellion signified nothing for him but self-indulgence and waste. The man's entitled to his opinion, and there may be more than a few grains of truth in it. But this was also the generation that ushered in be-bop jazz, and the writing of William Burroughs. Are either of those any less worthwhile, or stimulating, than a pulp crime or horror novel?

Psycho II , the novel, opens with Norman as a librarian in the prison hospital. *"He wasn't crazy anymore... Of course, no-one is crazy nowadays. No-one, whatever he may do, is a maniac."* Norman has found a staunch ally in his psyciatrist, a Dr. Claiborne, who, despite Bloch's reasonable disdain for his profession, has *"found a way to reach him in the darkness"*. The good doc encourages him to take part in amateur dramatics, and "the greatest thrill of all came", naturally, "when he took the lead in **Charley's Aunt**". In the first couple of chapters, Bloch admirably lets rip with misanthropy and black humor. When some nuns visit the institution, Norman finds himself having erotic fantasies about big-boned Sister Barbara. She's interested in him as a textbook case, but he murders her and makes his escape wearing her habit. Norman mirrors Ed Gein's supposed necrophilia when he rapes an old nun after her death (this is **much** more outrageous than the subsequent movie). From thereon, Norman is a killing machine, nothing more. The main character is Claiborne, getting embroiled in the world of Hollywood exploitation movies when called in to work as technical adviser on a film called Crazy Lady, about Norman. As Bloch states, "the novel takes place in a universe where a movie called **Psycho** doesn't exist." But it still intrudes on the novel's incidents - Mary Crane's murder is referred to as a slashing in the shower, and no physical description is given of Norman at all. No big deal, maybe. But Perkins' universally recognised psycho would be about 50 by this time, while Bloch's tubby transvestite would be more like 65. The

Norman character, which Bloch took pains to build, is jettisoned so completely he just becomes a shadowy figure with a knife, standing behind an elaborate plot. Despite all this, and the (well-handled) spurts of violence which punctuate the book, the author still feels able to have his cake and eat it:

"There was a hell of a lot less homicide fifty years ago. And what there was mainly went on among professional criminals. Now it's amateur night - student terrorists, kids on the street, all competing for status by slaughter. Because our films, our television, our books and plays tell them that violence is rewarding."

It's gratifying that Mr. Bloch was honest enough to include books, anyway.

Despite early frissons like the necrophile rape, the author is quaintly shy of profanities - *"lousy mothersuckers"* is not the most convincing street-talk you'll ever hear. Meanwhile, the Norman Bates character, described by his doctor as a conscience-stricken and extremely unhappy man, murders several people in the first couple of chapters without consideration or afterthought. Before the book is halfway through, he fades away completely. It was this undervaluing of his own immortal creation that led Universal to reject the idea. They knew the audience would only be interested in Norman - what other angle to the Psycho movies could there be?

In **Psycho II** (the movie), written by Tom Holland of **Fright Night** repute, Norman is home to stay, and is definitely the most sympathetic character in the film. Holland, and Australian director Richard Franklin (who made a psycho-thriller called **Road Games** with Janet Leigh's daughter, Jamie Lee Curtis), release him from the asylum after 22 years of therapy. He's ready to rejoin society, but, wouldya believe it, some people just won't forgive and forget. Lila Loomis (Vera Miles, from the original cast), sister of Marion Crane, organises a petition to get him reinstitutionalized. The motel is being run as a sleazejoint by the new manager (Dennis Franz, alias Norm Buntz from **Hill Street Blues**). And his trusting young friend Mary (Meg Tilley), from the diner where he works, is really Lila's daughter and is conspiring to drive him mad again. While staying at the Bates place, she keeps a chair against the doorknob - her bedtime reading being **"In the Belly of the Beast"**, the memoirs of killer Jack Henry Abbott. Far removed from Bloch's slash-kill cop-out, Norman is the ultimate innocent in this celluloid sequel. Sure, murders take place all around him, rapid-fire but fairly graphic - Lila Loomis is pinned to the floor by a blade through her big mouth, the Franz character takes one in the eye. But we know that Norman's not really to blame, even if he is up to his old tricks. Mother's voice is getting louder again, and her little boy is confused, "You smell like the toasted cheese sandwiches my mother used to make me when I had a temperature", he tells Mary as the past comes howling back. By the end of the film, Mary has taken the rap for the murders (and a couple of police bullets). Norman is left to go home, to encounter the killer. She's a sweet old lady, not long out of the bughatch herself, who claims to be Norman's real mother. We know things are reassuringly back on track when our hero clubs her with a shovel, she collapsing like a Tex Avery cartoon character. As credits are about to roll, we hear Mother's voice telling Norman "Turn me to the windows, I want to keep my eyes on you."

As a sequel to a bona fide classic, **Psycho II** is pretty commendable. As director Franklin says, it wasn't meant to be a pastiche, but in the spirit of Hitchcock's original film. Disappointed buffs who found it too jokey overlooked the point that Hitchcock made **Psycho** as a tongue-in-cheek comedy anyhow, though you **do** have to have a pretty black sense of humour to see it...

Perkins was happy with the sequel, honing the aging Norman's nuances to an angst-ridden point. "Perhaps Two is enough", he openly reflected at the time. "I don't think we should mine the territory for every last bit of gold dust. It would be nice to leave some of the story unspoken."

Noble sentiments, but no-one believed 'em. Least of all Tony Perkins, so it seems.

In '86, Norman was back, with a spiky post-punk haircut, in **Psycho III**. Written by one Charles Hinton Green, it was directed by Perkins himself. Maybe there was more gold dust in the mine than first anticipated.

Even jokier than its predecessor, this one is well into the realms of pastiche. Norman spends most of the film making allusions to his past misdeeds. A drifting greaser comes by to look for work at the motel, claiming "I won't be staying around too long".

"No-one ever does", remarks Norman. He saves a suicidal young ex-nun from taking her own life - "I guess I did make a mess" (of the bathroom), the wrist slasher admits, embarassed.

"I've seen it worse", he says. It's with this fellow neurotic that he finally finds love. Naturally, it's all due to end in tragedy. Going rapidly out-of-kilter, he notches up his highest body count to date. In full "Mother" mode, he slashes up someone's hapless, horny girlfriend in a telephone booth - a very spiky variation on the shower scene. ("Mother... Oh God, blood, blood!", he screams when he's back as Norman - one of many direct echoes from the first film.)

By the end, when almost everyone bar him has been murdered, Norman goes to his mother's mummified corpse and literally rips the stuffing out of her. "Why d'ya do this to yourself?... They're gonna lock you up forever this time", scolds the sheriff.

"At least I'll be free", he retorts as he's led away. The ultimate shot shows him smiling psychotically exactly as per the first Psycho. It's pretty much an '80's re-run of that first film - more irony, more violence, more sex, more cynicism.

The Psycho series made its last stand in 1990. **Psycho IV - The Beginning** is a made-for-cable movie, also released on video in Europe. Considering its origins, it could have been worse.

Its flashback sequences have a Geinian resonance, showing the origins of Norman's oedipal problems. Olivia Hussey is a surprisingly young and attractive Norma Bates (she only ever grew old in Norman's mind, as her mummified corpse rotted). Her young son is already the obsessive, watching her throw a neurotic fit through the famous "Marion Crane" peephole. During a spot of playful wrestling, Mother gives Norman a hard-on, then punishes him by dressing him as a girl and locking him in the cupboard.

What weakens the whole show is the main plot device (despite a script by original screenwriter Stefano). Norman has contacted a phone-in show about matricidal killers, spilling the beans under the pseudonym of "Ed". He's now out on release again, married to his psychiatrist (!), and believes he's about to have a relapse. No-one ever said movies were real life, but fer chrissake... When the latest reminscences of murder are added to his tally, Norman seems to have killed only slightly less people than Union Carbide. And now, within a few short years of his last committment, he's out and shacked up in matrimony with his old lady shrink?

It was fortunate that the series stopped here - the greatness of the first movie (or two), and the novel, are undiminished, the appeal of the character preserved. Had the series not ended, it would now have been rendered redundant by the sad death of Anthony Perkins - an underused actor, rarely called upon to exploit his deep intensity in any role other than that of Norman. He'll be missed by this movie fan, and many, many more of us.

Chapter Two
BILLY & HIS PA

**This chapter is testament to the
endearing ineptitude of the
exploitation film industry.**

Billy and his Pa are not so much the offspring of Ed Gein
(whatever their creator might claim), as the afterbirth of Norman
Bates.

In 1973, small-time auteur William Girdler made a movie called
Three on a Meathook. Filmed in Louisville, Kentucky, on a
budget of good will and a bucket of blood, it is a wonder to
behold.

Soon as the eerie, pseudo-jazz theme tune ends, we know what
we're in for. A good-looking blonde woman and a rough-looking
guy are in bed. Rather like the lovers' tryst at the beginning of
Psycho, only here there's nudity (and no apparent acting ability).
She's going up to the hills for the weekend (though every scene is
filmed on flat ground) with her girlfriends, three equally groovy
'70's chicks. Could it be, you ask at this point, that the director's
going to build up audience identification with her, only her to kill
her off after a couple of reels?

Well, almost. Soon as they get to the godforsaken nowhere
they're headed for, they break down and are taken to the farmstead of Billy Townsend (James Pickett), a kind of funky-
sideburned Norman with camera shyness. Billy lives with Pa
(Charles Kissinger), and Pa has warned him many times - "You
know what happens when you get around women!" We can all
guess.

Before we've had a chance to identify with any of 'em, the girls
are all massacred. Girdler clearly likes to climax early. There's a
gory sub-Psycho bath stabbing, a bloody shot-gun rampage, and
an effective decapitation. Girdler may not be cinematically
competent enough to direct a registry office wedding video, but

he clearly knows how to spill blood.

After Billy wakes and realises things are going wrong, he travels to his mom's grave: "Mom, I think I did something bad again. If I keep killing people, I oughta be in an institution, but Pa keeps saying it's gonna be okay." Ah, so a young guy's a mass murderer - he'll grow out of it, they all do.

Billy wanders the streets and bars, to some interminable "psychedelic soul" songs (called "You've Gotta Be Free" and "We're All Insane") by a bar band with pudding basin haircuts. A waitress picks him up - "You had an accident!", she tells him when he wakes up naked in bed with her, but it's not quite clear if he's wet the bed. Her acting is so blank it's almost *cine-verite*.

He wants to bring the waitress (Sherry) back to the farm with him, but Pa reminds him of the awful past. In a childhood flashback, he remembers being dragged off his bicycle by Pa, to be shown the first woman he'd murdered during a mental blackout. Darn kids - if it's not one thing's it's another.

But Sherry does come to the farm, and, what's more, she brings her blonde friend Becky with her. Cue interminable scenes of the three of them running through fields together. Becky keeps diving into the long grass, then springing up again, behaving in every way like an acid-addled muppet.

Later, Pa prepares dinner at the farmhouse for 'em. He's drunk and obnoxious, but he's rustled up his speciality. Veal - "Pa has a special way of smoking it." Don't he just. Straight from the Ed Gein cookbook.

While Billy and Sherry go for after-dinner sex, Pa, the ol' buzzard, puts a pickaxe through Becky. Shock-horror - it was Pa all the time! When Sherry goes looking for her friend, she finds three naked girls hung on meathooks in the barn (hence the title, in case the subtleties escaped you). They confront Pa in the kitchen, where he's preparing more "veal". He poises to attack with his meat cleaver, when who should run in but Mom! Turns out she wasn't dead after all, though she only lasts a moment before Pa imbeds the blade in her.

Later, when Pa is glowering, just like Norman, in his padded cell, a "psychiatrist" gives a deeply profound interpretation of this troubled man's actions. Seems he was driven mad by acting as a procurer for Mom. This final summation goes even further than **Psycho**, in its psychiatric addresses to the layman - "When he learned the nature of her illness was cannibalistic, he should have had her institutionalized."

Words to be heeded. This is a movie with a message. It is beyond trash. It is surreal.

Three on a Meathook, devotees of arthouse cinema will be crushed to hear, has been out of circulation since the '70's. The producers, Studio One, had an injunction strapped on them for ripping off the poster artwork of a contemporary, much superior film. Namely, **The Texas Chainsaw Massacre**...

*T*hree on a Meathook

Chapter Three
LEATHERFACE

"The film you are about to see is an account of the tragedy which befell a group of five young people. In particular, Sally Hardesty, and her invalid brother, Franklyn. It is all the more tragic that they were young. But, had they lived very, very long lives, they could not have expected nor would they have wished to see as much of the mad and the macabre as they were to see on that day."

"**The Texas Chainsaw Massacre...** What happened is true! Now the movie that's just as real!" That's what the posters said. Anyone who knew better could have shaken their head, but facts and truth ain't always the same thing.

Though there's not a single character in the movie who is based on Ed Gein, the atmosphere and the details reflect his grimy life and crimes beautifully. **Chainsaw** is one of those pieces of independent cinema that just grow from a hill of sand. In 1973, hippyish young Texan moviemaker Tobe Hooper and his co-writer Kim Henkel were looking for a title that might grant them fame, or at least notoriety. Hooper was initially inspired by a group of his fellow Texans, flocking around the chainsaw section in a department store. Add this no-doubt potent image to the influence of **Night of the Living Dead**, E.C. horror comics, and a few unsavoury details from the life of Ed Gein, and what do you have?

A mouldering, rancid ragbag of a film is what you have. Something that either disturbs with its seedy insinuations of depravity, getting deep under the skin, or else disappoints with its lack of hi-tech flash. The acting is mostly amateurish, though spirited. The interior sets are apparently just places where the crew were able to set up without interference. The soundtrack consists of a mess of caterwauls, scrapes, and industrial noises. The special effects are primitive in the extreme.

*L*eatherface - **The Texas Chainsaw Massacre**

And the movie is terrifying. It is an icy punch in the guts.
It opens in a desecrated cemetary. A rotting, disintegrating
corpse is strapped to a graveyard monument. The camera pulls
slowly away, as a radio report crackles out its list of indignities
committed on the buried dead. Shades of ol' Ed, but there's much
more insanity to come.
We meet a minibus full of kids - late teens to early twenties -
who are heading out to the graveyard where the grandfather of
Sally (Marilyn Burns), and her crippled brother Franklyn (Paul
A. Partain) is buried. Along for the ride are Sally's boyfriend,
Jerry (Allen Danzigere), Pam (Teri McMinn) and Kirk (William
Vail). They may start out like the buddies in "Scooby-Doo", but
they end up the most terrorised, degraded group of bodies in the
cinema. On the way to the family farm, they pass a stinking
slaughterhouse, and a piece of "roadkill" (dead armadillo). Small
details, but then the whole claustrophobic atmosphere of the
movie relies on small details. They stop to pick up a seedy
looking hitchhiker, which is their first big mistake of the day - a
real fruitcake, a classic piece of psychotic over-acting. Edwin
Neal, an ensemble actor who got the part through simply "acting
crazy", based the character on his brain-damaged, schizophrenic
nephew. "I read the script, I said "that's him, that's Paul!'"
Texas must have been dumped on by a few truckloads of bad
acid, because this is one manic creep who makes you itch just by
being on the screen. His hair looks like it's never been washed,
and he has a long, purple birth mark down one side of his face.
As Neal says, "he's as far as it goes. He's second generation inbreeding." Franklyn lets him waylay them into a discussion on
slaughterhouses (it's the family trade, he was born into it). He
tells them about his brother's talent of boiling down the head of a
cow to make "headcheese". After trying to talk 'em into paying
two dollars each for some crummy polaroids, he demonstrates the
effectiveness of his pocket knife by drawing blood from his hand,
pushing the blade straight into his palm. This scene shows the
essence of the whole film. The grainy quality of the picture, the

naturalistic acting, everything makes it uncomfortably real. The viewers feel almost as trapped in the presence of this geek as the characters. And, almost unbelievably, the hand gouging scene is the bloodiest in the whole film. No-one literally sees any mutilation, any discernible eating of human flesh, any rending apart of young women, in **Texas Chainsaw**. But plenty of people think they do. In fact, there's less blood in this film overall than there was in **Psycho**, 14 years before. It's the cumulative effect of so many bizarre details which overwhelms many viewers. The traumatic whole is so much more effective than the usual stage-managed set pieces.

The next character they meet in this backwoods backwater is a garage owner (Jim Siedow), who also sells delicious barbecued sausage. Meat plays a progressively major role in the movie. When they get to grandpa's old house, they wander around the derelict property awhile. Kirk goes inside to investigate a strange buzzing sound he hears. As he calls out, the noise stops. But then a metal partition door slides open, and a huge body steps out. At least 200 pounds of bulk, menacing, with some kind of weird rawhide mask covering hs facial features... Leatherface, take a bow!!!

Hooper decided he wanted Swedish-American Gunnar Hansen for the part, as soon as he turned up for audition and filled the entire doorframe. The gentle giant was asked "Are you violent? Are you crazy?" He couldn't answer yes to either, but he could sure look like he was.

Leatherface - one of the hitchhiker's headcheese-lovin' brothers - is an even more frightening example of inbreeding. Pathetically dependent on his siblings, he's monstrously strong, childlike, and sadisitic, in equal quantities.

Mute, and presumably deformed (we never see his real face), he can only express himself with grunts, squeals, and violence. Hansen took himself to the grounds of a mental institution, and walked around studying seriously retarded inmates, before slipping on the hallowed mask. He was supposed to come up with a

124

voice for the hulking psycho himself, but couldn't find the right
tone. Hooper dubbed pig squeals over the soundtrack instead.
From the moment Leatherface hammers in Kirk's skull, totally
without hesitation, the movie hits a downward spiral of fatalistic
abandon. The only thing certain is the helplessness of the kids,
about whom the audience is made to care. It's quite different
from some Friday-the-13th type gore voyeurism. Because of the
convincingly mundane nature of these characters, and the way in
which the disturbing camera angles make you suffer these at-
tacks, rather than just witness them (see the shower scene in
Psycho), you're with them 'til the bitter end. One of the most
notorious scenes of the film occurs when Leatherface grabs hold
of the hysterical Pam, carries her screaming into the butchery
room (where Kirk lies dead on the table), casually drops her on a
meathook, then walks away to attend to business. It's this kind of
callousness that makes watching vegetarians feel smug. What's
most unbearable about the scene is the way Pam kicks, gasps and
chokes while she's on the hook. This is preceded by a short plop
of punctured flesh as the big guy lets her drop. Hideous.
But the horror's all in the mind. As Edwin Neal says, "I have
won bet after bet with people who claim you see the hook go
right through..." In fact, the hook is neither seen to enter nor
leave the flesh. The scene was simply effected by stopping the
camera, standing Teri McMinn (Pam) on a soapbox, fitting a
harness on her to raise her slightly above it, reversing the hook
and getting 'em rolling again.
But the hysterical pitch never surrenders itself, and the audience
can be persuaded that they're seeing anything.
The real meat of the film occurs in the scenes where Sally is
tormented. For these alone, the British censor has banned the
film from re-release (cinema or video) on the grounds of "psychological torture". By the time she remains as the only survivor,
she's trapped in the house and finds an old couple upstairs. An
old, mummified, **dead** couple. A plucky (not to mention
desparate) kid, she jumps from an upstairs window. In-

jured, she manages to make it to the gas station, but tarnation, wouldn't ya just know it, folks round here is all related an' all. The barbecue man may be the sanest and most capable member of the family, but he has his nasty quirks. Driving her back over to the house, he can't resist digging and poking her with a broom. Hooper had to encourage Jim Siedow, a gentlemanly, middle-aged Texan, to really beat Marilyn Burns. There was no time and no room for fakery. He didn't like the idea, but she encouraged him. Eventually, he really got into it, and Marily fainted after the eighth take. Of all the actors - and most of 'em found the film a riveting but unpleasant experience - she suffered the most. At the end of production, here skin was a mass of cuts, scratches and bruises, almost mirroring the way she ended up on screen.

The most effective and unnerving scene comes when Sally slowly regains consciousness. Everything seems calm, as he eyes slowly open and her vision pans around. We could be party to that ancient cinematic cop-out, the bad dream. But no. Horror comes screaming back at her all at once. She's in a room filled with human bones. A fat chicken clucks out its misery from the confines of a birdcage. She's tied to an armchair - literally, the armrests are human limbs - and the family are apoplectic with glee at her distress. The decrepit old man she assumed was dead is in fact their 102-year old Grandpa. He's the most highly regarded of all the slaughtermen, and he's gonna do for her in "the old-fashioned way". They hold her pretty, hysterical head over a steel tub, while Grandpa fumbles the clawhammer, never bringing the expected blow down. Instead, they cut her finger, and let the rancid old bastard suck on it.

Like the man said - psychological torture.

The dinner scene is the hellish highlight of the whole film. It occupies nearly five minutes on screen, and took thirty hours to shoot. The same meat remained on the table all the time, and was decaying rapidly. The "human" skeletons were set on fire by the lights. The headcheese was rotten after only one hour, and people occaisionally had to hold up a take to go and puke. As

*E*dwin Neal/*M*arilyn Burns

Edwin Neal says, "the movie was shot at a temperature of 155 degrees. It became easier to take on the part as we got into the **environmental** aspects of the movie."

One particular Geinian moment at the dinner table occurs when Leatherface comes in wearing one of his alternate faces, a "pretty woman" mask. More highly coloured than the others, it's the result of an excised scene where he slaps bright lipstick over it. At the end of the movie, Sally escapes alive, but with her nerves in shreds. It's little wonder that the prologue to the eventual sequel spoke of her "escaping from a window in hell", and being committed to a mental asylum for the rest of her short life.

The effects of Texas Chainsaw were phenomenal. For a low-budget movie, the profits were immense. Of this, however, relatively little was seen by the director, and none by the actors, all revenue split among a mess of distribution deals.

Many people thought it was the most disgusting thing they'd seen, and wouldn't be budged from their conviction that the violence on screen was explicity detailed. Gunnar Hansen even recalls being told by "some old dowager type" that "there were twelve people murdered today in New York, Gunnar, and it's your fault". It opened the door for the flow of more intense, or simply more gory, horror movies. Some have tried to match the tension of **Texas Chainsaw** just by using special effects, which dooms them to failure. **Chainsaw** caused controversy wherever it was shown (previously, the most hardcore psycho-horror film had been Wes Craven's **The Last House on the Left**, but that was rarely granted a showing anywhere). In Britain, it was banned everywhere except in London, where the Greater London Council granted it an X certificate (adults only). This same GLC would ban The Sex Pistols from playing, two years hence, but was liberal enough to allow a horror film with a distinctly anti-social, punk attitude (seminal New York punk band The Ramones sang a tribute called **Chainsaw** on their first album, while many other bands used imagery from the film, most commonly the Leatherface masks).

The movie became a dark cinematic icon, like **Psycho**, though of a much seedier kind. There was never any attempt to make a sequel until the mid-80's, when Tobe Hooper made himself available for the project. His career had got off to a promising start, followed up with more slabs of American Gothic - **Death Trap, Salem's Lot, The Funhouse.** In the '80's, he seemed to lose his way, getting tied up with much blander projects than he'd made his name with. Still, if anyone could pull off **The Texas Chainsaw Massacre Part II**, it was him. That the film disappointed a lot of people was largely due to historical factors. It was outrageous enough to be banned in a few places (like Britain, predictably). There was violence aplenty, like the brain-skewering of obnoxious yuppies, and the added psycho-presence of Dennis Hopper as a vengeful sheriff. But, to some, its black humour was too much like light relief, whereas only the sickest of individuals could bring themselves to laugh along with Leatherface's family in the first film. After the first movie, there could never be any return to days of innocence. By its very existence, it meant that nothing was ever going to disturb in that way again, unless it was absolutely, emotionally devastating.

In '89, **Leatherface (Texas Chainsaw Massacre III)** ran the audience through the (chain)sawmill again. Basically, it was an effects-heavy re-run of the first film. The violence was intense, and exceptionally graphic (banned in Britain, natch). One notable addition to the family was a little girl who carries the corpse of a baby around as a doll. As the long-suffering heroine is made to watch her boyfriend's torture (she being nailed by her hands to a table), the child begs Leatherface not to go through with it. After the heroine gasps a frantic sigh of relief, the brat sneers "You said I could kill 'em next time!"

But, for most of the audience, nothing can exceed that first whiff of rancid headcheese. Leatherface is a trademark for children's toys in the USA now (masks, model kits, etc.), like that other cuddly serial killer, Freddie Krueger. He has his own comic book, and has moved, only a short step, from being a symbol of the unthinkable to a figure of popular culture. Much like the man who part-inspired the original Southern Gothic film in the first place - Ed Gein.

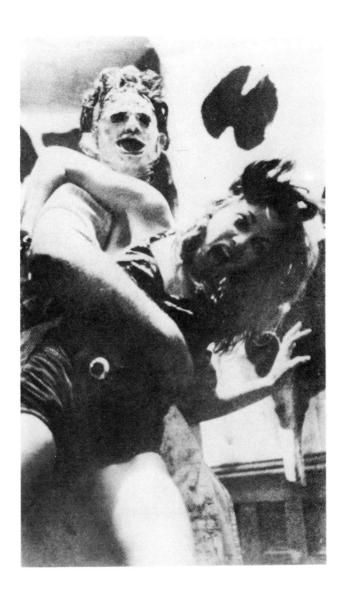

*T*he infamous meahook scene

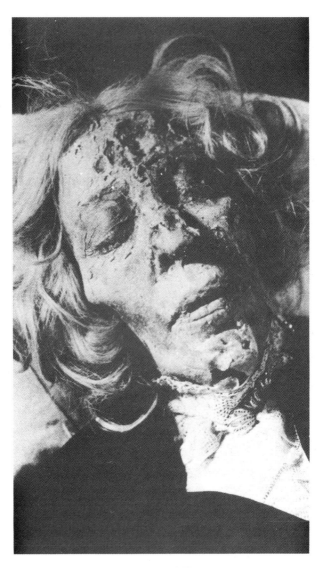

*E*z's Mama - from **D**eranged

"This is a human horror story - perhaps we can learn something from it. Something of our own fears and nightmares."

If **The Texas Chainsaw Massacre** had one major negative effect, it was that it all but covered the tracks of **Deranged**, a 1974 offering from American International Pictures, written and directed by Alan **(Children Shouldn't Play With Dead Things)** Ormsby. When Ed Gein attended his sanity hearing that year, he would have had no knowledge of two movies in progress based on his crimes. The first, we've already spoken about at length. The second, **Deranged**, was a gruesome black comedy, which tells a story you may just find a little familiar.

It opens with a silly, po-faced introduction by Tom Sims, "a newspaper columnist from the hometown of Ezra Cobb". As the theme music (church organ) plays, we're transported to the home of "Ez" and his Mama, "Amanda". Ez's father died when he was 10, since when Amanda an' him have worked the farm. Now she's dying, and she's scared to leave her innocent, "young" (approximately 48) son to the mercy of all the gold diggers in the world - "You're still a handsome young man, Ez. You have a great attraction to the opposite sex." Ez is played by Roberts Blossom, thin-faced pinhead supreme. Mama advises that "Maureen Selby's the only woman I ever trusted - she's fat, that's why!" As she starts to expire, she also reminds Ez that "the wages of sin is gonorrhea, syphilis and death!" Simple-minded innocent that he is, he can't accept her passing, and, in a sickly funny scene, spoons pea soup down her 'til she pukes up a bubble of blood.

"Still Ezra refused to accept the death of his mother", narrates Sims, hovering omnipresently like Rod Serling in **The Twilight Zone**. Ez writes letters to Mama every day, and keeps a dress with a frying pan face on her bed. Eventually, he resolves to

cure his loneliness the Norman Bates way, when he hears Mama
calling from the cemetary. "Perhaps, in his twisted mind, he
thought she would look the way she did in life", comments Sims.
This illusion is shattered when he pulls her rotten arm off. Still,
on the way home in the pick-up truck, Ez is happy as a pig in
shit, singing "She's the Girl of My Dreams" in a maniacal howl.
But when he gets home, he realises just what bad shape she's in.
"Now he intended to restore her - he tried to re-patch her with
fish skin, wax, anything he thought resembled human flesh."
His good neighbor an' protector Harlan Cootes (the movie's
Lester Hill figure) inadvertently gives him the idea to use other
corpses when he mentions the obituary of their old schoolmistress, Miss Johnson. Ez has never heard of the obituary column
before, and is pleased as punch to find some useful informatiion
that beats the sports pages. Sure enough, up comes Miss Johnson
from the soil that night.
After Harlan and his wife take Ez aside for a talk about the birds
an' the bees, Ez, who says "Yes sir/yes ma/am" more than Elvis
ever did, puts on his best straw hat and goes out to court the
eccentric Maureen Selby. She's yearning for her deceased husband, Herbert, and wants to organise a four-way seance so that
the two of them and their loved ones can all come together.
Back home, he speaks with Mama about his new ladyfriend.
"She is fat, Mama, just like you said - but I like that fat!... Only
thing that bothers me - I don't know if she's all there in the upstairs."
But that woman has got filth on her mind. When she conducts
her seance, she tries Ez on by reporting that "Herbert says he
misses the carnal side of our relationship".
"Carnival?", queries Ez.
When they get right down to business, Mama's hollerin' in his ear
about the wages of sin. So, naturally, he fires some shots through
Maureen's head. She goes home to join his expanding family.
The touch of female flesh has intrigued Ez, though, and he starts
seeking female companionship. "Her name was Mary Ransom",

Sims tells us, "and, truth be known, she was a little over the hill. But she was beautiful, she was promiscuous, and Ez had never seen a woman like her before." She's actually a good-looking, gypsyish bar waitress, who gets Ez drunk for the first time in his life. Soon enough, Ez is getting his own wicked ideas, and he tricks her into accepting a ride from him. Back at Ez's place, she finds herself keeping company with with Mama, ol' Miss Johnson, Maureen and Ez himself, bedecked in human skin. "Everyone's lookin' forward to meetin' you - they think you're a real fine girl... make me a real good wife." He makes her attend dinner with the corpses, tied up to a chair (and touched up - he's getting very lecherous). Best of all, he acquaints her with the assistance they all offer him: "They help me make things - see that violin, that's not catgut!" He bangs out a rhythm with his bellydrum and legbone, with which he bloodily caves Mary's skull in when she tries to escape.

Out in Harlan's yard, the two old schoolfriends have a familiar exchange:

"That Mary Whatstername?... Don't they know they're never gonna find her?"

"She's not missin'... I got her back at home."

The opening day of hunting season finds Ez and Harlan in the store where Sally, the girlfriend of Harlan's son, works. Harlan is trying to get Ez interested in the rifles, but he doesn't want to go hunting. "I don't like all that stuff." He has other plans.

When the hunters have gone, he shoots Sally in the face, grazing her and knocking her out. She escapes from the pick-up, but he stalks her through the snowy woods like a deer, 'til her foot's ensnared in a trap.

Back at the store, with Sally missing, Harlan's on expresses the belief that Ez has hurt her and robbed the store. His father flies into a rage: "I tell ya, Ez would never do anythin' like that - I've known him 35 years!"

Meanwhile, Ez strings Sally up for the oft-censored gutting scene. In the uncut print of the film, blood pours copiously down over her naked breasts. As Harlan, his son and the sheriff close in on him, Ez starts singing a hymn, then descends into gibberish. The frame freezes with him wailing his head off. The last word, of course, belongs to Tom Sims:

"Several nights later, under cover of darkness, a group of townspeople reputedly led by Harlan Cootes burned the Cobb farmhouse to the ground."

Deranged is a rare, sleazy little gem. It turns up every now and then at midnight movie screenings or on cable TV- try to see it if you can. Any resemblance to persons living or dead is simply because they're too far gone to care.

Deranged

*L*ux *I*nterior at *P*lainfield *C*emetary

ED'S EPITAPH
by
Lux Interior
of
The Cramps

When the startled cops busted in the door to Eddy Gein's bad-lookin, horror-worn house and took a look inside, what to their bulgin', wondering' eyes should appear amidst the debry on the floor but two **Startling Detective** magazines. What they found next would top anything Ed ever giggled over in **Startling Detective.**

They'd already found what they came lookin' for in a shed connected to to the back of the house. The last hunk o' "venison" Eddy brought down with a 22-calibur bullet. It was opening day of hunting season and her name was Bernice. The trophies they found, which contributed to the ambulance ambience of the place, included:

bracelets made of human skin; four human noses in a cup on the kitchen table; a pair of human lips on a string dangelin' from the windowsill; strips of human skin covering four chairs; a tom tom made from a coffee can, with human skin stretched over the top and bottom; a pair of leggings made from human skin; skin from a woman's torso converted into a vest; nine death masks - the skinned faces of women - mounted on the walls; ten heads of women sawed off above the eyebrows; another head converted into a soup bowl; a purse with handles made of human skin; a refridgerator stocked with human organs - frozen; a human heart in a pan on the stove; a belt made of human nipples; a four-poster bed with a skull on top of each post; a waste basket made of human skin, and a lampshade made of human skin.

...And dancin'! He was a dancin' fool! He knew it takes two tits to tango, so he'd put on all these girl parts - strap 'em on good and tight - and run around in the yard, bang his tom tom, and raise hell! That Eddy, what a guy! He could play squeezebox as well as tom toms (the King of Rock and Roll!). And he was loaded with jokes too - only the town quit laughin' when they found out his jokin' were't jokin'.

"Them cops done flubbed their dub on that Mary Hogan murder. She's over in my house right now!" Har Har Hardy Har Har! What a party guy.

He was always there when the townsfolk needed a babysitter (he loved children - little girls, rare). He had his own code of good moral sex - no sex with corpses he dug up from the cemetary, 'cause they smelled too bad".

No-one went hungry in Plainfield, with Ed always diggin' up free gift packages of "venison" for 'em. He was an all-round good neighbor.

If you really want a thrill, quit fantasizin' about going to Texas to see that house where they filmed **Texas Chainsaw Massacre**, and go sit in Ed's yard in Plainfield, Wisconsin. It's two hours smack dab in the middle of no place, but it's worth it. The ground is so soft you sink into it six inches, 'cause when the local vigilante group burned down the house they just lit and split, and no-one ever goes around there. The foundation of the house still sticks up (except for seventy-five pounds of it we took with us when we left - about got a hernia carryin' that out!). You can still feel the terror there. The land is flat as far as you can urinate. I seen Ed dancin' and beatin' his tom tom right there. I said "Hi Ed", and he said "Hi Lux". But I probably said both of them.

I asked this hillbilly burnin' leaves about half a mile away where it was, , and when I realised by the look on his face that all of our black vinyl and leather stuff was horrifyin' him, I became horrifed at where I was myself. We was standin' there horrifyin; each other for a while - not knowing what to do, when he just pointed and said "Over there". I said "Is it where there's a shed, way in the back?" He said "Yep". I said "Thanks", and backed off.

Oh yeah, this is an epitaph, so I would have to say at this

point: there are many good men, but few great men. Ed was a great man, but not a good man. Eddy the digger - he's much bigger than you.

Chapter Five
ED GEIN - A HERO FOR OUR TIMES?

**"When he got home with the dead girl it was midmorning...
He took off all her clothes and looked at her, inspecting her
body carefully, as if he would see how she were made."
CHILD OF GOD - Cormac McCarthy**

As you'll glean by stealing a peek at the preceding epitaph, by
Lux of the Cramps, popular myth has given ol' Ed a change of
image - from unspeakable criminal to cult hero.

Time has lent us the safety of distance from his crimes, especially
in his homeland, where he contaminated the undergrowth of what
was supposed to be a time of security, of Mom's apple pie, and
strong family values (on the surface, at least, though things are
never truly what they seem on the surface). Before Ed Gein
started to creep his way into popular culture, Cormac McCarthy,
the great Southern Gothic author, wrote the sorry tale of Lester
Ballard, a Tennessee backwoodsman. In **"Child of God"**,
McCarthy's 1973 novel, young Ballard is a man all gone to seed.
Evicted from his old family home, he takes to living in a rundown shack, living off a diet of tasteless cornbread, with the
stuffed animals he wins at a fairground rifle range as his only
companions. Grinding hardship, and the world's total indiffer-
ence to his human needs, force him into a rapid descent. With
his shack burned out, he takes to living in a cave, shooting young
women dead and robbing graves to procure bodies for sex. By
the time he's eventually apprehended, his cave is populated by
dead women in advanced stages of putrefication. Committed to a
state mental hospital, he spends the rest of his life "in a cage next
door but one to a demented gentleman who used to open folks'
skulls and eat the brains inside with a spoon."

The character certainly isn't Ed Gein (Ballard is an embittered
and disliked outcast all the way through, making his alienation
even more understandable than Ed's), but the stories share

enough elements to call into question whether such a powerful work would have been created without knowledge of the Gein case. McCarthy invites sympathy for Ballard, by unsentimentally depicting the total bleakness of his existence, at the same time making him repulsive with matter-of-fact descriptions of his crimes. The author sets out to illustrate, and succeeds in doing so, just what depths an isolated soul can reach. The story also has an element of regional folk tale, the blackness of the text made readable by McCarthy's sparsely poetic, Southern narrative. It's these mythic elements, more than anything else, that call to mind the legends of Ed Gein, legends that have long since entered the mainstream of popular culture.

Back in the late '50's, Lois Higgens, President of the International Association of Policewomen, drew a highly individual moral from the Gein case. According to her, Ed's insanity was solely due to a "short course in murder, cannibalism, necrophilia and sadism" given by crime magazines and horror comics. She warned the legions of upright, credulous young mothers she addressed that horror comics would be the ruination of their children. This was in 1957, you understand, three years after they'd been legally banned anyway. Let's all applaud the fall in the American crime rate that resulted.

In the late 1970's, the Comics Code Authority, which had held sway over the industry since the moral panic of the mid-50's, started to lose its hold. There was already a thriving underground comix market, with Ed Gein starting to exert a fascination over many of the artists and writers as a symbol of the ultimate social transgressions (see illustrations accompanying this chapter). Gradually, many of 'em would turn pro, as the '80's saw most of the "dangerous" young people put their creative talents into comics, instead of the increasingly conservative rock 'n' roll industry. Among these was Rick Veitch, who created a strip called **Mama's Bwah**. Despite its claim to be the "real story behind **Psycho** and **The Texas Chainsaw Massacre**", this was

a cartoon romp, pitting Leatherface against a gang of delinquent Archies. The mythic elements of the Gein case were becoming official folklore. In the same mag (**Weird Trips** - a special issue on ol' Ed), an artist named William Stout gave an excellent pastiche of the classic '50's horror comix. If you look carefully at our repro, you'll see Leatherface and the Old Witch, one of the E.C. horror comic narrators, staring out from Ed's cupboard. To the American comic artists, these were Ed's truest contemporaries. They were among the first people to regard him less as a criminal than a trash culture phenomenon of the '50's, just like **Tales From the Crypt** or **I Was A Teenage Werewolf**. Ed continues to provide subject matter for comic book artists up to this day, with at least one "True Crime" series planned which will take a far more factual approach to the Gein case, amongst other uglies.

In the late-70's/early- 80's, the rush of splatter and "slasher" movies made the occaisional foray into the psychology of the mother obsessive. Most of these were plasma-colour derivatives of Norman Bates - like the pathetic Donny (Dan Grimaldi) in **Don't Go In The House**. Donny keeps the corpse of his religious fanatic mother in his apartment (but you knew that, didn't you?), and, as a consequence of her nasty habit of burning his arms when he'd misbehaved as a child, enjoys nothing better than bringing a young woman home and frying her alive. You can make up the rest yourselves. The only notable aspect of the film is the very end, when a child-beating mother is seen to be preparing her abused kid to join the next generation of serial killers (over-simplified, okay).

At the hardcore end of the spectrum, only William Lustig's **Maniac** looked at the loneliness and nihillism of the oedipal killer straight on, without any cinematic gloss. It's possibly the most extreme movie to use the talents of SFX man Tom Savini, and certainly the most hated. Garrottings, decapitations, shootings, scalpings (a particularly nasty Geinian touch, with the murderer's scalp collection adorning tailor's mannequins) - all

*M*aniac

were shown ultra-realistically from the point of view of the killer. More fantastic were the hallucinated return of his nagging mother from the grave, and the revenge of his numerous victims. **Maniac** was the most subjective, non-judgemental look through the eyes of a murderer up until John MacNaughton directed **Henry: Portrait of a Serial Killer** in 1986. Given the above, and the convincing nature of the violence, it was too much for most viewers to take. Richard Meyers, author of the book on exploitation cinema **"For One Week Only"**, called it "the single most reprehensible film ever made", with only Chas Balun stepping up to defend it on the basis of its sheer nerve.

By the time **Henry** came to be a cult hit at the beginning of the '90's, the subject of serial killers was receiving serious treatment and had become big news (and will probably remain so, given the course that present day history seems to be taking). The mainstream was starting to embrace the dark and the unthinkable, as demonstrated by little rich kid novelist Brett Easton Ellis's **"American Psycho"**, the subject of one of the best planned negative publicity campaigns in recent history. Supposedly a satire on consumer society, it seems to lovingly embrace most of the values it sets out to lambast, ending up as a well-written eulogy to perverse sex, violence and FM rock music. The anti-hero, Patrick Malahide, is a fervent materialist, a Wall Street broker, a real child of the '80's. But even he can get a vicarious thrill from a small-town iconoclast like Ed:

"After a deliberate pause I say, "Do you know what Ed Gein said about women?"

"So what did Ed say, Hamlin asks, interested.

"He said", I begin, "When I see a pretty girl walking down the street I think two things. One part of me wants to take her out and talk to her and be real nice and sweet and treat her right." I stop, finish my J&B in one swallow.

"What does the other part of him think?", Hamlin asks tentatively.

"What her head would look like on a stick", I say."

The influence of the Gein case over media depictions of the serial killer phenomenon almost makes an irrelevance of the question of whether Ed Gein actually **was** a serial killer. After all, there is only verification that he ever killed two women - hideous enough, but this makes him a double murderer, rather than a counterpart of our own present day creeps who go all out for double figures, in an effort to win the Nobel Prize for Psycho Killing. Given the evidence that he may also have been responsible for the disappearance of two teenage girls, it may be that he fits the definition (although even these events, tied together with the murders of the older women, would have given a leisurely time span of 10 years for his crimes).

It can also be argued that his lack of rational motivation welcomes him to the serial killers' club. True enough, but he's still a world away from the prolific "king for a day" type who taunts the police in a cat-&-mouse battle of wits, or the sexual sadist who kills purely to achieve some sick sexual gratification. If all the evidence, personal testimony, case history, and outright myth (and, of course, this book) are to be believed, then Ed Gein was skinning and killing in order to achieve some magical change in his very being. In his alienated, deluded mind, he searched for, and almost found, a personal transcendence which would free him from his own identity, his own sex, from the very world he lived in.

It's this psychological element which has been so ingeniously seized on by crime fiction writer (and former crime reporter) Thomas Harris. In "**Red Dragon**", the first of his novels featuring the sociopathic genius Hannibal "the Cannibal" Lecter, a vile serial killer at large, nicknamed "the Tooth Fairy", berates one of his victims for not being able to see what he is "becoming". The theme is developed further in the immensely popular "**Silence of the Lambs**". Here, FBI agent Clarice Starling tries to pick Lecter's pathological brain to find clues as to the identity of "Buffalo Bill". Bill is so-called because he "likes to skin his humps". Like Ed, he murders for the most peculiar of reasons.

He's a skin transvestite.

"What is the first and principal thing he does, what need does he serve by killing?", Dr. Lecter asks of Clarice.

"Anger, social resentment, sexual frus-".

"No."

"What, then?"

"He covets. In fact he covets being the very thing you are."

It's little surprise to know that Thomas Harris was a 19-year old, trainee crime reporter when the Gein story broke. In Jonathan Demme's movie adaptation of **The Silence of the Lambs** (remarkable on many counts, not least for the sympathy for the victims the audience is made to feel, via the compassion reflected by Jodie Foster's tender/tough performance), Ted Levine gives a bravura, but largely unsung, performance as the grotesque Jame Gumb, otherwise known as Buffalo Bill. Prancing around his living room in wig and make-up that makes him look like a slap-painted heavy metal star, this resentful, deep-voiced wannabe-woman holds his dick between his legs, effecting a magical Geinian transformation.

It's the power of **Silence of the Lambs** which has effected a certain vogueish belief in the serial killer's actions being a ritual of metamorphosis (I've largely subscribed to this myself in my telling of the Gein story). No-one should take it to be a rule - the only rule about serial killers seems to be the presence of a distorted ego. But if we accept that most people want to escape the limitations of their existence in some way (whether by playing football, turning the TV set on, or taking a shot of heroin), then we must realise that some people will go (<u>have to</u> go?) to far greater lengths than others to achieve this. And if we're this close to diagnosing a condition, might we not be partway there to prescribing a cure?

If Ed Gein lived in present-day society, might he not have found the release he needed in a sex-change operation? (Buffalo Bill doesn't, which causes his resentment to grow further). If imaginative solutions, rather than literal ones, are needed, might not Ed have played out his fantasies as a sartorial transvestite, maybe bringing his morbid interest in the female body and his creative dexterity together by working on some kind of gynaecological "body art" (after all, how far was Ed's upholstery job from the famous Allan Jones "woman chair" that so enraged feminists?). It's all so logical, and it's all blatant baloney. The world is not Greenwich Village. Given the choices of an extreme, irreversible operation, and a life of camping it up as a way-out artist in a small mid-western town, most Ed Geins would still find grave robbery and murder a safer, easier option.

Anyhow, today Ed is none of the above. Today, he's a rock 'n' roll star.
Back around the time of Ed's committment, Bunny Gibbons, carnival huckster of Rockford, Illinois, paid $760 for Ed Gein's '49 Ford Sedan. One born every minute, you say?...
Think again. It was a sound business proposition. Made its first public appearance in July 1958, at the Outgamie County Fair in Seymour, Wisconsin. **"See the car that hauled the dead from their graves! You read it in "Life" magazine! It's here! Ed Gein's crime car! $1,000 reward if not true!"**
Ed Gein's car roared its way around the mid-west, making money for Bunny. It was the first acknowledgement that there was easy cash to be made from Ed's sickness. Ed's motor kept on rollin', and it wound its way into Manhattan just past the turn of the '80's.
Ed Gein's Car - cute name for a pop group, eh? - was a post-punk, New York hardcore band, wreaking apocalypse at a high decibel level. Something had happened to the counter-culture mentality since Ed was incarcerated two-and-a-half decades earlier. The beats started off diggin' poets, modern novelists, and stone-cool black jazz players. The hippies were into mystics, avant garde film makers, rock stars and "psychic explorers". The punks, and their immediate descendants, went for anyone with a fierce, anti-social attitude.

In personality terms, their heroes were the polar opposite to our Eddie... but then, his actions always did speak louder than his words. In the disillusioned, post-punk era, young people were looking for social aliens they could identify with.

Not the traditional "rebel". That was too '60's. Rebels need a cause - -they need a consensus, no matter how radical. The more spaced-out, non-conformist hippies might embrace a shyster like Charlie Manson, but not a misfit like Ed.

But if there was an impetus to American post-punk youth, it wasn't idealism, it was nihilism. Step right up, Eddie Gein.

Kids were no longer interested in the illusion of coming together and changing the world. If they felt alienated, then they wanted to stress that separateness. All the distance they felt between themselves, their families, and every other human stiff they ever encountered. If that gulf couldn't be bridged, and if that distance bred murder... **so whadda fuck?**

Alienation was what they identified with. Total alienation seemed oh-so-romantic.

Now, punk rock seems as far away as the days when Elvis first raped a microphone. But an increasing number of keepers of the rock 'n' roll flame have found themselves identifying with Ed Gein every bit as much as (or more than) they do the Memphis Flash.

The Cramps, those trebly, psychotronic wildcats, were the first band to truly raise Ed to the status of a rock 'n' roll icon. Lux Interior, their whoopin'-an'-a-hollerin' frontman, has said that his visit to the burned-out Gein farmstead (described in **Ed's Epi-taph**, in this book) was a greater moment for him than seeing the Beatles for the first time on the Ed Sullivan Show. Lux has no qualms about owning up to be a genuine "Ed Gein fan". He seems to see in him a genuine love of outrage, a kitschy '50's style, and a gift for over-the-top schlock horror (true-life horror, it's true, but we're talking personal interpretations here) that makes him just as much a seminal rock 'n' roll artist as, oh, Bo Diddley. Lux, together with his fellow Cramp and lover Ivy

153

Rorschach, to pen an uptempo tribute to Ed, the year after he died. **People Ain't No Good** appears on the album **A Date With Elvis**, their finest two sides of trad rock 'n' roll gone psycho. Complete with an infants' choir on the chorus, Lux's hiccuppin' vocal makes the merest allusion to Ed (*"They're no good for weekends/when they come out to play./They're no good for bookends/'cos you can't make 'em stay"*) Namecheck comes in the fade-out, when Lux starts speaking in a Texas Chainsaw drawl: "Eddie's dead now too - there just ain't no barbecue... I'll just have some of those porker lips."

The song's followed straight up by What's Inside A Girl - a wild song that wears its heart in it's shorts, but has lyrics that might fit a certain frustrated Wisconsin farmer:

"There's some things, baby, I just can't swallow/Mama told me that girls are hollow/Uh-uh... What's Inside a girl?/Somethin' tells me there's whole nuther world... In the bottom of your bottomless bodypit/You got somethin' and I gotta get it."

The Cramps gave the cue for a whole hellish legion of metal, hardcore noise and psychobilly (beery Cramps imitators without the melody) bands to record their less-than-ambiguous tributes. The almost comically morbid thrash metal band, Macabre, issued the song **Ed Gein** on their **Grim Reality** album:

"I make bracelets out of bodies/And coffee can drums made with flesh/Organs frying in my kitchen/And the skin off your chest is my vest."

Okay, so the lyrics don't exactly give a new perspective, but they're veritable masterpieces compared to their more minimal songs (which are all concerned with murder and/or death). Try **Exhumer** for size:

"Taking off your jewlry/And having such a ball./I'll take it to the pawn shop/And I'll sell it fuckin' all!"

Or their tribute to **Son of Sam**, on the same album:

"I am Sam; death in hand/I would not like green eggs and ham."

Ain't those little rhyming couplets just impossible sometimes? Tad, the Seattle noise rock band, recorded the song **Nipple Belt**

An Ed Gein fanzine

Part of the cover from Macabre's **Grim Reality** album

for their 1989 album, **God's Balls**. Against a background of high-pitched, chaotic guitar noise, singer Tad Doyle intones cute little statements such as *"My name's Ed Gein - got a heart cookin' on my stove", "I need some anti-freeze/to keep my women young",* and *"I love the girls that I wear."* It's infinitely more menacing than the Macabre piece, mainly because we can hear a black sense of humour at work (and it's mostly intelligible).

Since then, more Gein songs have rolled out of garages and small concert halls all over the land (psychobilly band The Meteors actually issued an album called **Mad Man Roll** with a close-up of Gein's face on the cover). Most amusingly, they've served to fuel the paranoid suspicions of some parents that any kids who are not on crack or ecstasy are on a death kick.

The simple truth is that Ed Gein is now as much a part of the folk culture of many young people as Santa Claus was when they were small. Howls of protestation about how unhealthy it is will do no good at all (this writer, for one, has been called a "dirty, fucking, evil pervert" by a politically right-on warehouse man who objected to the first edition of this book - having the "wrong attitudes" is the same as being a murderer, as any politically correct person will tell you). Ed exerts a fascination, not simply because he was horribly cruel to women. The point of his crimes was not sadism, else his victims wouldn't have been quickly dispatched with one shot to the head. What simultaneously enthrals and appals about Ed is that the things he did just don't seem possible. The imagery of his crimes seems dredged up from some surreal nightmare: the skin suit, the flesh furniture, the bone ornaments. There's something primal about Ed Gein that will always remain in the recesses of the popular conscious-ness. Only 35 years on, his story has taken on the resonance of a darkly mythic folk tale; or even a scary fairytale -

"Once upon a time, there was lonely little pixie named Ed, who used to carry fat ladies away from their homes so that he could steal their skins and look like them..."

That's why I'm not too alarmed when young people, with no

(apparent) homicidal inclinations, tell me, without any hint of irony, that they're "Ed Gein fans" (this goes for girls, too). They are captivated by a true story that's grown into a popular myth, in the same way they might be by a paperback novel or a fiction-based horror movie.

A decade after his death, Ed is a figure of popular culture. In the US, kids can now buy latex Ed Gein masks, which reproduce his homely features in pale rubber, with a few scars and shadows to make him look ghoulish. You can also collect Ed Gein Fan Club ephemera (t-shirts, badges, coasters, et al). The originator of this merchandise is currently engaged in making the first film about ol' Ed to look at the case straight on, without fictionalization. He promises me that "we'll show everything, nothing will be left out". I don't know whether to cheer or gag, but I appreciate his reasons for doing this - dark fascination.

In this age of random slaughter, we use Edward Gein as light entertainment.

Select Bibliography:

"Deviant " - Harold Schecter
**"Edward Gein - America's Most Bizarre
Mass Murderer"**
- Judge Robert H. Gollmar
"Psychopathia Sexualis" - R. Von Krafft-Ebing
Gray's Anatomy
"Psycho" - Robert Bloch
"Child of God" - Cormac McCarthy
"The Silence of the Lambs" - Thomas Harris
"American Psycho" - Brett Easton Ellis

ED GEIN FAN CLUB (MERCHANDISE):
FOXX ENTERTAINMENT ENTERPRISES
7752 JAMISON AVENUE
RESEDA
CALIFORNIA 91355
USA.

NEMESIS BOOKS
EVERYTHING YOU WANTED TO KNOW,
BUT WERE TOO SCARED TO ASK.

Coming soon, to a brave bookshop near you:

TRUE CRIME - the most compelling case histories.

CULT MOVIES - the wildest movie books you've ever seen.

STRANGER THAN FICTION - think you know the world you live in? You ain't seen nothing yet.

CRIME FICTION - the toughest new crime around.

If you want to know more about Nemesis Books, send a stamped, addressed envelope to:
Nemesis
Unit 4
Millmead Business Centre
Mill Mead Road
London N17 9QU.

NEMESIS -
THERE AIN'T NO RECESSION IN MADNESS